BLACK
HEART
—— *of* ——
CHINA

LEN TITOW

SWEETSPIRE LITERATURE
——— MANAGEMENT ———

CHAPTER 1

Ling Fu, a girl three years of age, walks down a wide path between two sets of houses in her village. A convoy of six military trucks and two tanks makes a thundering noise as they enter the village of Chan Low, disturbing its peace.

The girl is stricken by fear at such a sight. She panics, screams, and tries to turn and run back home. The driver of the truck does not slow down or stop to allow the girl to get out of the way and just runs right over the top of her. The tank behind in convoy follows the truck and runs over the body of the girl in defiance, crushing her small body into the earth below.

The girl's mother comes out to see where her princes is and begins screaming hysterically for other members of the village to help find her little princes.

The convoy moves into the centre of the village and after they have passed by, a leg is visible protruding from the ground beneath.

The mother runs to the crushed body of her little daughter, weeping hysterically while other members of the village come out to help dig the body of her child from the earth that opened to take her.

Soldiers jump out of the back of the trucks and round up the villagers and direct them into the centre of the compound to hear what their captain has to say. They order everyone to move to the centre, but no one is listening as everyone is trying to dig out the buried girl.

A soldier hits one of the older villagers with the butt of his rifle, sending him to the ground while pushing the others to leave the girl and get to the assembly to hear what they have to say.

Some villages resist and refuse to co-operate and are shot. The soldiers make it clear they do not care for human life, especially uneducated peasants that form the majority in the Chinese provinces.

The mother, weeping hysterically, refuses to leave her daughter and continues digging, hoping she is still alive.

The captain comes up to her and draws his pistol and shoots her in the head at point blank range, killing her instantly. Others immediately stop digging and get to their feet and move to where the assembly has gathered.

Life means nothing to the Chinese, especially when it is someone else's. A cultural attitude that has developed nationally with those in authority.

Captain says, 'We understand that James Chu and his family came from here. He has fled Hong Kong, and we believe he is seeking asylum in a western country. We understand his parents are from this village and know where he has fled. We want to speak to his parents and anyone else that may know of his whereabouts. If you do not co-operate, we will arrest you and send you to the mines.'

'Who knows where his parents live?'

No one speaks, and everyone is afraid of the military and says nothing. You do not enter a village with such force unless the motive is to kill many. The military knows the villages do not carry arms, so why else would they come with such force? Purely as a tool to intimidate the villagers and if necessary, kill those that openly object to their authority.

The captain says, 'Since you will not co-operate, we will search every house and if we find the parents, then we will arrest them and their neighbours for not co-operating. I have warned you.'

A thin elderly man steps forward and introduces himself. 'I am the father of James Chu, but I do not know where he is. The last I heard he was in Hong Kong protesting the Government who refuse to allow Hong Kong's independence.'

Captain says, 'You're lying. You know where he is, and you will tell us. Arrest him and all his family and load them into the truck. We will take them with us. What about the rest of you? Have you heard where he is?'

No one steps forward or says a word.

James Chu's parents, his brother's and sister's family are also loaded up into the truck along with neighbours. Twenty-three are bundled up and forced against their will to be transported to Beijing.

Captain says, 'If we find you a withholding information, then we will be back with force, so it would be wise to tell us now.'

No one came forward, so the captain gave the order to move out and the convoy began its long journey to Tan How Military Base. Once there, all prisoners were escorted by four guards to holding cells.

The next morning, one by one, each was taken out of their cells and interrogated by the military police from Peking. This went on for days and at the end of the week a report was broadcasted, that prisoners that were taken from the Chan Low Village, had tried to perform a mass escape and the military had no choice but to open fire on them killing all twenty-seven prisoners.

CHAPTER 2

Three months prior to the arrest, James Chu left Hong Kong to pay a visit to his parents at Chan Low. He and his wife made the trip, leaving their children with his wife's parents in Hong Kong.

To ensure the police would not arrest them, they moved to the mainland as tourists. They were aware the authorities knew about their advocacy for Hong Kong's freedom and independence from China. They also knew that the Government would soon prevent them from protesting further.

They would flee from the Communists and seek an asylum in a western democratic country where they could speak freely and operated under the Rule of Law. This would be the last time they would get to see their parents. James knew it was too risky to bring the children with them, as they might be arrested and thrown into prison on a cropped-up charge.

The truth was not something the Chinese Government wanted to hear or uphold. They broadcast what they want the people to believe in, not the truth, and this disbelief makes the people fear the Government, as they know what is said are lies, to make the Government look good. Best say nothing or do nothing contrary, otherwise you will be dealt with severely? Spies in each village report to the police and action is taken swiftly, without warning, should a report be made.

James and Suzanne Chu moved into a house they knew was empty as the occupants had been arrested and never heard of again. Their children who live in Hong Kong went underground as they knew they were being investigated and would also be arrested and dealt with as their parents were. Their parents were involved in publishing a community paper which had printed stories about the Government and what they were doing to the Muslim minority in China. The Government wanted them to repeal the story and to print a story that most of the Muslim population voluntarily went into camp to learn about the Chinese Governments objection to their teachings and to set them on a better path to success and voluntary participation in transforming their society into a more productive one for China. They knew that this meant the Muslims either adopted the Government's stand on religion or face the consequences of elimination, as had been the case of the Hindu and Buddhist religion in China.

The villagers allowed James and his wife to move in on the understanding that if arrested, they would not reveal the whereabouts of the owner's children.

After setting up occupancy in the house and staying there for a week, James, under nightfall, went to his father's village and met with his mother and father in a tearful reunion. They agreed it would be too dangerous for Suzanne to come to the village as it would attract attention. James never stayed more than a few hours and then went back to his home while it was still dark.

James never met with his cousins, aunts, uncles, as this would put them in danger should things get out of hand in the Hong Kong demonstrations. China would arrest his relatives and force James to capitulate, or his family would pay the penalty for his actions. The Chinese are a race of people who have little regards for anyone else's life, only their own. As for human rights, well, no one cares about this in China and your right to any aspect of life depends on your wealth and position held in government and not in society.

James arranged for his parents to come over one morning, giving them enough time to meet and talk and for his parents to get back to their village that evening, without attracting attention.

Suzanne was in tears as she met her in-laws, for she knew that there will be little time for them to spend together.

After the traditional formalities, the four sat down to tea and to discuss what had happened in Hong Kong and the possibility of the world intervening in the Hong Kong demonstrations. China had not ordered the military into Hong Kong but declared its tolerance was being stretched and soon would order sweeping political changes.

China had considered that the situation would defuse itself and military intervention was unnecessary. However, they were prepared to take the risk.

The Chines believed if the world allowed them to get away with establishing a naval base in international waters in the South China Sea, then they could get away with anything that they did, as they would have the right and military strength to back up any action they may contemplate taking, and no country in the world would dare to oppose them.

In the past, the Chinese felt sub-servant to the rest of the world. Under its President it wanted to change this image and wanted to be the envy of the world and not only this but most important feared as a nation.

James brought his father up to date on what they were doing in Hong Kong and that they were fighting for their democratic rights, which China was opposing. China demanded they transition to a Communist State and adopt the laws of the mainland. The residents of Hong Kong opposed this and came out to protest China's policy.

It became obvious as the conversation progressed that James had a problem, which he was hesitant to raise with his father. This continued until his father asked him straight out, was he willing to risk the life of his parents and family to achieve independence, for there was little doubt that the Chinese would act against the family of those who opposed their control.

James knew he had to confront this question as it would come to be the key element to be decided upon by not only him but all the protesters; whether they continued their fight for democracy or capitulate and knelt before the communist regime.

His father was visually upset and tried to hold back the tears. He knew James had to make an important decision not only for his personal safety, but for the existence of those they would leave behind, for the communists were not a forgiving government. The decision James wanted his father to help him make was, is the movement worth the lives of his parents, uncles and aunts and their children and the parents and children of those protesting?

James's parents could not help him decide and shortly after made their last farewell and left in tears, knowing this was the last time they would ever see their son and daughter-in-law.

James and his wife stayed for another day, then made their long journey back to Hong Kong. They knew their decision was vital to the existence of their outer family and therefore decided not to continue protesting but to leave Hong Kong and seek an asylum in a Western Country that protected a person's democratic rights.

CHAPTER 3

I t was midnight. James and his family were on board a plan headed for Australia. The Government declared they would welcome entrepreneurs and professionals from Hong Kong into their country and would support and assist in their application for citizenship. On board were thirty other families who were also granted entry visas, and who were told they would receive government support in becoming citizens.

The Chinese Government expressed their vehement opposition to Australia's decision to accept these individuals and grant them democratic rights and freedom to move around the country while their residency applications are pending.

China demanded that these individuals be sent back to Hong Kong to face charges as they viewed them as criminals. They threatened to consider any country supporting them as an enemy if they refused to comply with their demands.

James and his family received help from the Australian Government with housing, schooling, and banking to establish themselves in Australia.

Some that migrated were professional people who were given the right to hold a licence to practice upon demonstrating they held qualifications in their field of expertise. Those in doubt were helped to gain a licence to practice by being allowed to sit for exams, which were arranged on short notice. Most could set themselves up in practice as lawyers, accountants and medical practitioners and live the free life they tried to do in Hong Kong but were prevented by the Communists.

James, who was a heart specialist, bought into an established practice with three other doctors from Hong Kong. Over time, he bought a home in an established area and moved his children from state school to a private school. His wife, also a professional person, a lawyer, found employment with a large legal firm who specialised in human rights, environmental issues, and international law.

Things were working out for the Chu family and, in fact, for all of those who came to Australia following the clampdown by Chinese authorities in Hong Kong. They prospered from establishing themselves in practice and became recognised members of society.

Within the Chinese community existed several individuals that held allegiance to China, and these individuals would report back to the Government as to what was happening in Australia and how these new arrivals were settling in Australia.

The Chinese, back in China, did not report the truth but advised on State Television that all the immigrants found they were not welcomed in Australia and, because of Australia's racist attitude towards the Chinese, could not find housing or work. They declared they were destitute and have applied to return to Hong Kong for resettlement. The Chinese Government declared they viewed these people as traitors and would not accept them back into China and if they got back to Hong Kong, they would be tried and either shot or sent to prison for their treachery.

Six months past; James received several emails from loyal friends in China that his parents and the other members of his family and his wife's family were arrested and taken into camp shortly after he and his family fled Hong Kong. They were reported shot dead trying to make an escape from a detention centre. Of course, this was a fabrication of the truth as his father was in his seventies and had arthritis in the hips and knees preventing him from moving quickly or even trying to escape. This was an outright killing of innocent lives, but the Chinese cared little for the truth or what the world thought of their version of events.

All the other families that fled Hong Kong received the same news that they killed their loved ones in trying to escape the detention centre, and authorities, who declared they were fearful for their lives, opened fire to defend themselves.

The Australian Government, upon hearing of these murders, arranged a press conference and openly declared they would seek an explanation and press the matter before the United Nations demanding an investigation. They received support from the European nations and from Canada and America. The nations of North Korea and Russia supported China, but the world knew of China's attitude towards freedom of speech and human rights. China vetoed Australia's move to have the matter investigated by an independent investigator who were to report their findings to the United Nations Commission on Human Rights.

James, upon hearing that all his family were killed, sobbed uncontrollably, and had to be admitted to hospital as he collapsed in shock and had to be sedated. He was in hospital for about a week on various antidepressants and was released with a referral to see a psychiatrist. They made an appointment for him, which he kept.

The psychiatrist took his time to find out the root of the problem and got a pathology test of James's body chemistry through blood and urine samples. He put James on a course of mild medication for depression and made appointments for further sessions with James over the coming weeks.

Psychiatrist said, 'James, what you have I believe is the Black Dog Syndrome. It is in fact depression, and it does not respect the person but usually is brought on due to stress of modern living or sometimes caused by the person being genuinely unhappy with themselves.'

'Depression is used to describe a range of emotions and conditions from momentary unhappy to suicidal despair. It is a debilitating condition. It varies in intensity and duration, but the physical, mental, and spiritual factors are always present.'

'The cause of depression can be many of which the main ones are:

1. Biological changes in the body chemistry that contribute to mood disorders.

2. Physical Factors.
    (a) Chemical or hormonal imbalance,
    (b) Some physical diseases seem to induce depressive tendencies,
    (c) Hereditary factors,
    (d) Endogenous causes -a disease.
3. Temperament'

'There is a total loss of identity. You no longer know who you are. That is why it is easy for a depressed person to commit suicide.'

'Psychologists often describe depression as a mood disorder, a state characterised by a sense of inadequacy, a feeling of despondency, a decrease in activity and reactivity, pessimism, sadness, and related symptoms. They often describe it as the "Black Cloud of Despair". A feeling of total exhaustion. An abdication of responsibility.'

'Those that have depression often describe what they see in greys, blacks and white. They seem to have lost colours.'

'Depression is most likely to occur in adults of the ages of 45 to 65. Initially, described as major depression disorder or MDD. This is the most common mental health condition.'

'Depression differs from being sad. Sadness is a normal condition of humankind from time to time, but depression is more constant. It is a serious mood disorder that can negatively affect your health and quality of life, and those closest to you. The fifth edition of the Diagnostic and Statistical Manual of Mental Health Disorders (DSM-V) states depression is recognised where there is a period of at least two weeks when a person experiences a depressed mood or loss of interest or pleasure in daily activities and had most specified symptoms, such as problems with sleeping, eating, energy, concentration or self- worth. This definition does not include grief, which you experienced with the death of your parents.'

'Most people who have depression try not to have it diagnosed and just live their lives with the condition. Those with the condition often let it go for months before speaking to their doctors or seeking medical help. If left untreated, depreciation can stick around for years and can lead to suicide, and even if it goes, it can come back.'

'There is no one cause for the onset of depression because a combination of genetic, biological, environmental, and spiritual factors all plays a role. There are differences between men and women with depression.'

'Women are likely to worry, dwell on, or rehash negative feelings which appear as sudden crying spells, feeling guilty or blaming oneself. They are more likely to have depression at the same time as an anxiety disorder, such as panic disorder, eating disorder or obsessive-compulsive behaviour.'

'Men are more likely to show signs of irritability, anger, apathy or spend more time at work than required or show reckless behaviour such as misusing alcohol or other substances.'

'Mostly, depression is diagnosed by your local doctor through a survey. The replies given to a questionnaire can note the severity of the depression. Most doctors would follow this up with a blood test to rule out things that could masquerade as depression, such as an underactive thyroid.'

'Recovery is a journey, not a destination. Bad days still occur, but with treatment, you should be able to cope. While science has not yet found a cure for depression, it is possible to live a happy and fulfilling life despite it.'

'As stated previously, you should not mix depression up with sadness, which is a normal emotion that everyone will experience in time. A specific situation or event usually causes it, such as losing a job, the end of a relationship, or the death of a loved one. With depression, the person feels sad or hopeless about everything. They may have every reason on earth to be happy, yet they lose the ability to experience joy or pleasure.'

'With sadness you may feel down in the dumps for a day, but you can still enjoy simple things like your favourite TV show, food, or spend time with friends. This is not the case when someone is dealing with depression. Even events or activities that were once enjoyable are no longer interesting or pleasurable.'

'When you experience sadness, you can still sleep, remain motivated to do things, and maintain your desire to eat. Depression is associated with serious disruption of normal eating and sleeping patterns and not wanting to get out of bed, staying all day.'

'In sadness, you might feel regret or remorse for something you said or did, but you will not experience any permanent sense of worthlessness or guilt as you may with depression. One of the diagnostic features of depression is this kind of self-diminishing, negative thought patterns.'

'Finally, self-harm and suicidal inclinations do not arise from non-depressive sadness. Those struggling with severe depression may have thoughts of self-harm, death, or suicide, or have a suicide plan.'

'Many people assume that if you ask someone if they have suicide thoughts, that you can put the idea into their head. Mental health professionals recommend asking questions and gathering facts to help someone who is depressed or feeling hopeless, despite myths that suggest otherwise.'

'When someone is contemplating suicide, their words and actions can give you clues that they are at risk of hurting themselves. Key indicators are:

- Isolating from others.
- Not communicating with friends or family.
- Giving away possessions or writing a will.
- Driving recklessly.
- Increased aggression.
- Increased drug and alcohol use.
- Searching about suicide on the internet.
- Gathering materials such as pills, drugs, or weapons.'

CHAPTER 4

James sat in his study, looking at the bare wall. He thought about his parents and what he had done to them. His action was the cause as to why the Chinese killed them, his uncle, aunts, and their children. All gone. Every one of them killed in cold blood. Even his nephew, who was only three years old. If he did it differently, they would still be alive. If he acted sensibly, they would still be alive. He should have listened to his father. What did he and all the other demonstrators achieve? Nothing. They showed they were a violent mob wanting democracy, knowing the Chinese would never capitulate. He knew the Chinese had no appreciation for life. This was clearly shown at Tiananmen Square protest in 1989 when tanks were brought in to massacre the protesters.

James sat staring at the wall. Not even blinking. How could he have done it differently? He demonstrated, thinking the democratic world would support those in Hong Kong and prevent China from having its own way. The free nations should have supported them in their fight to become a democratic country. No. No one came to their aid. All that they did was pay lip service and allow the Chinese to move in a crush their cause.

It would be different if his parents and others gave up their lives for a cause that finally was won, but this was not the case. No matter how much they protested. It all meant nothing. They lost the cause, and their relatives were killed for nothing.

Everyone who lived in mainland China and Hong Kong knew what the Chinese were capable of, and that life meant nothing to the Communist Government. All that they were concerned with was their image of being seen as a strong leadership. The President was on trial, as were the demonstrators, and the President wanted to prove he had the strength and character to make the tough decisions, and if this meant the loss of life, then so be it.

James stared at the wall, trying to get the guilt from his mind. He was trying to blame the Chinese Government for it was they who ordered the death of his relatives and not him. Yet he could not escape the fact that he knew what they were like and knew the risk was great. They had hoped to get world support for their cause. In reflection, this was a foolish hope, as the world would prefer to allow China to claim Hong Kong as theirs rather than lose trade with them. The money was too important to them. The lives of a few protesters, compared to a trade agreement, were not worth getting upset over even if it was Hong Kong, the financial capital of the world.

The world sat back regards Hong Kong and allowed it to be taken over by the communists. A democracy since 1898 and now a communist state.

All for nothing other than a hope and a reliance on the world backing up what they preached, namely Hong Kong, should be for the people and not the Communist Government's territorial rights.

James sat staring at the wall, looking into a black deep hollow, thinking only about the deaths of his parents, all the other relatives. He could only think about them while staring into the black deep hole. His thought shifted momentarily to Taiwan. Do you think the promises other countries gave to support Taiwan would be honoured? James didn't think so. They will end up the same way as Hong Kong. Left to defend for themselves against the military and economic might of China.

CHAPTER 5

John Bishop is a minister at St. John's church. He came from an average working-class background and worked as a psychologist for ten years before entering the ministry.

He receives a lot of jabs in that he works at St John's church as a bishop and some parishioners still believe it is his church, and several of them have referred to him as a saint. A lot of his time is spent on dispelling rumours about him and his church. He doesn't meet with parishioners who have psychological issues and directs them to other psychologists. He focuses on the spiritual problems of the parishioner.

When the spiritual problems are more important than the psychological ones, he makes an exception.

He sits in his study looking over the file Dr Hyneman had sent him regards James Chu and his summation of James's situation and condition. He advises he has placed James on a course of medication designed to ease his depression and concludes the problem lies more with the soul and not the mind.

John reads the notes and scans through the chemistry analysis, which appears normal, and which confirms James's problem is not a chemical imbalance but a psychological or spiritual one at the cause of the depression.

James arrived on time and was taken to John's office and asked to wait. About ten minutes later, John appears and introduces himself and both go into John's study, where James is shown a chair and takes a seat.

John says, 'James, it is a pleasure to meet you and I understand you are currently being treated by Dr. Hyneman for your depression. Dr Hyneman, with your authority, was kind enough to provide me with a copy of his clinical notes and it explains your background and that you are blaming yourself for the death of your parents, uncles and aunts and their children.'

'You believe they would still be alive if you had not left Hong Kong?'

'He advises your condition is not improving and you cannot get on top of your guilt complex and most of your time is spent staring at blank walls or at nothing, which he describes as a typical "The Black Dog Syndrome".'

'Is there anything you wish to add to Dr Hyneman's report?'

James says, 'No. You just about covered everything. It was always weighing up of our lives against the cause and most in the protest movement felt the cause was worth it, but only a few stood up while the rest refused to get involved. So now, we are being punished because we were against the Communist Party and tried to get support from the rest of the free world and our own people in Hong Kong. China could divide and conquer us because the majority did not come out to support us and because other countries did not want to get involved or feared what China would do to them politically and economically. My father warned me what would happen if we continued fighting for democracy. But we thought that the cause was worthy of a few lives and still believe this, as long as it was not our lives that had to pay the price.'

John says, 'So, it was a fight for democracy and freedom which was totally opposite to the political system existing in China.'

James says, 'Yes, but we felt that since we had been under British rule for many years that the Chinese would allow us independence. We now know this is a foolish dream, as China will never allow this and give up its territory. It would prefer to eliminate the people there rather than give up its sovereign rights to the territory.'

'My parents said that China would never allow independence. However, we believed that with international support, we could persuade China to allow Hong Kong to gain independence, but this was not the case. America did not want to force the issue with China, nor did any other nation. We were betrayed by the world, who gave every indication they would support our cause, but when the time came, all they gave us was lip service. We were left on our own and were crushed. My parents and the other supporters' relatives were killed for a cause, which now does not exist and was for nothing. We basically gambled their lives away. We lost.'

John says, 'James, are you a christian?'

James replies, 'I believed in God, but we don't go to church. My wife went regularly with the children. But she now has doubts about the existence of God and believes the Communist Party was correct, as God has done nothing to come to our aid or support us in our move to gain independence. He has allowed the Chinese to conquer Hong Kong and to kill all those innocent people who maintain their stand against freedom.'

John said, 'God does not run governments, but has left mankind to do this. He will take control when he returns and has left man to develop the kingdom of heaven on this earth. So, it is humanity that is at fault here and not God. You and others leave it to God to do your work for you and when things go bad or do not go your way, it is God who gets the blame.'

'You want to do something and when it does not turn out the way you want it to go, you blame God. What you are saying is you are God dictating what must be done and God, in your belief, is there to do as you command of Him otherwise, in your mind he does not exist.'

'I am sure Dr Hyneman has told you that depression is a medical issue, a psychological issue, and a spiritual issue. Sometimes, it is a permutation of all three.'

'In your case, Dr Hyneman believes the death of your parents and relatives at the hands of the Chinese is playing on your mind but not sufficient as to cause depression. He believes your soul is the problem and has therefore asked me to see if I can help you.'

'James, we know extraordinarily little about depression, except for the Christians. We know it is a great trial because, most times, faith and feeling conflict with each other. The problem with depression is that most times, people feel they have no possibility of getting better or that no one cares about them, nor will anyone help them; so they feel the only way out is to commit suicide.'

'They reach this point when they feel they have failed. In these instances, they should seek God's help rather than trying to cope with the problem on their own. Sometimes, they consider God but reject him and commit suicide because they do not know enough about God and believe He would reject them rather than help them. They do not consider why he died on the cross and what this means. They should seek God instead of contemplating suicide and should discuss their condition with their family and local doctor. The more they open up about their condition, the more people can help. Keeping their depression a secret does not help anyone, least their family or close friends.'

'This is one of the greatest problems that Christians face when dealing with depression. We can accept that our bodies and mind will undergo stress and conflict as we go through life, but for the christian it is considered our faith will rise above such things but most times it does not, and the depression becomes more intensified.'

'Even if you cannot feel God present, I can assure you He is there and you should have faith in Him, no matter what happens. During your depression, do whatever you consider pleases the Lord and you will find things to take a turn for the better.'

'Christians become depressed because their present has lost its meaning and purpose, and their future holds no hope. This is because the christian has a living relationship with God in Jesus Christ, and the glorious anticipation of the resurrection and second coming dissipates as the condition takes hold and the christian loses his belief in Christ.'

'The thinking here is, if God refused to come to my help, then I cannot rely on Him for anything in the future and therefore all the preaching about the resurrection and second coming will not happen or if they do, then I am considered by God as an outsider and will not take part when it comes. He believes God rejects him, or at least he is being ignored.'

'In these instances, the point the Christian is missing here is that they were placed on this earth to serve God and not the other way around. The Bible states "ask and it shall be given". This does not mean right away, and you should have faith in Him, that just because God did not intervene immediately when you wanted Him to, as he has a better plan and will right all wrongs. You should have faith in Jesus Christ in these instances rather than dropping your bundle and say, "O well that's that and God will do nothing for me".'

'The christian's depressed condition seems to stand in direct conflict with their faith. They reach a point where they question their faith as a christian. "Why me Lord" is commonly uttered as well as "Why didn't you come to my aid, Lord?'

'Consider Moses and the forty-year journey in the wilderness and you get a glimpse of what depression is like. Here, the Israelites did not believe in God, yet He shepherded them for the full forty years. He fed them by praying to God, who provided them with manna and water and looked after them during their walk in the wilderness. The same occurs when you have depression. You may not feel God's presence, but He is there looking after you and making sure you are heading in the right direction. The only thing he asks of you is to have faith in Him. Things may get worst then what they were before, but He asks you have faith in Him. Speak to Him in your prays and ask for guidance and His blessing and He will always be with you and ensure you come out on top of that debilitating illness.'

'Despair is a reaction to evil, the forces that work against the good of humanity. A brain disorder may involuntarily cause it, or it may be voluntary caused by giving in under the burden of too much pain. But it is always a reaction to some form of evil, some deprivation of the good and can overcome the christian faith.'

'The counterpart to despair is hope, which is optimism and when there is no hope, then the christian's world collapses and he follows the way of this world and becomes a disciple of Satin.'

'They often bury salvation through intense feeling of guilt, doubt, and fear and in your case, the feeling of guilt in not listening to your father, and believing everything was going to turn out all right, but it didn't.'

'Of what you told me about your parents, they were your idles, and to you they were God. They provided you with everything and you would always seek their guidance on issues, and they were there always to provide for and help you. In fact, you idolised them. They were your golden calf to worship. In your heart, they took the place of God and became God.'

'You believe you gambled the lives of your family and lost and cannot find peace in your soul, as your family is not around for you to seek their forgiveness. You acted despite knowing the consequences but didn't expect China to follow through with their threats. You were aware of the risks and culture of the Communist Party. It is their principle that counts and not their people.'

'People they have many and their policy is they must control these with an iron fist, otherwise the people will seek democracy in place of dictatorship.'

'Their death at the hands of the Communists means your God (parents) have been destroyed and now you do not have anyone to consult on these matters.'

'It could be said, in fact, that you have a serious conflict going on between your mind and your soul. Your mind wants to speak to your parents and seek their forgiveness while your soul reaches out to the real God to help you in these traumatic situations.'

'James, who is going to win the conflict between your mind and soul? That unfortunately is the conflict which is specially made harder by you not seeking the real God, for He is the only one who can help you in this situation. He alone only knows what your soul is experiencing and how it is to be satisfied. He is the only one who knows what it will take to bring you back to health and prosperity, for in situations which you are experiencing all the money on earth will not fix the problem for you. All that it will do is empty your pockets and allow some to take advantage of you.'

'Some see religion as taking care of the spirit when we are about to die and all other things are considered, such as wealth, materialism, while we are alive. The problem here is that the accumulation of wealth and materialism increases your sinful activity, so when you come to die, you have sinned quite a bit. You will not have your sins forgiven by just uttering the words "God, please forgive my sins". It takes a lifetime to prove your faith in Jesus Christ. Trials test you to prove to yourself that you either have faith and to what degree.'

'There is little doubt that you and your wife are experiencing the onset of trials that will be extreme, but remember, the Lord would not put you on this path without first making sure you were up to it.'

'Both of you gave up your religion not for a sinful act but for a cause that you and your people in Hong Kong wanted. The cause was greater to you than your belief in God. You decided it was wrong what the British Government did in handing back Hong Kong to China and therefore, you were going to take things into your own hands irrespective of the consequences. Those of you that had belief put it aside and instead of asking God for his help and direction, you took matters into your own hands and decide to act violently against the Government of Hong Kong who represented China. Because of your action, China took control, which caused you to flee to save your lives.'

'There is little doubt that even if you remained in Hong Kong that you would end up being killed and what had happened to your family would still have happened as China wanted to show the world and its people how it handles these situations and to show to Taiwan what will happen to that country should it follow Hong Kong and resist the communists.'

'I can do nothing for you as you have come here on the recommendation of Dr Hyneman and not to seek God. When your parents died, so did your God. Again, you thought you would turn up and during the conversation I would put my hands on you and utter a pray which would make you better, but of course that has not been the case. As a minister, I do not deal with magic, for that is for the devil to handle. The soul still wants answers, but whatever I say will not be accepted by you, and you will still end up being dissatisfied with my advice. The problem is in your soul and the disconnect of it with the real God. You cannot get back on your feet until you find God, which may not happen as I fear your rejection of Him is as a result that God did not follow your instructions.'

'To seek God is not just looking in the cupboard for Him. God is reaching out to you, but you are not receptive to his calling. Your mind is concentrating entirely on your guilt and your soul is trying to tell you to speak to God about your problem while your mind, which is governing your thinking, is telling you it is all your fault and there is no way out. You cannot bring your parents back. They were your God, so that is the end of the saga. You had human gods instead of the spiritual God.'

'It is not the end, for the one who created your parents is God. This, it seems, you do not wish to recognise. This happened for a purpose, which only he knows. He uses bad for good. He is the only one that can turn disasters into something good. They killed your parents for a purpose. Allow Him to show you why and, in the processes, you can find faith in Him.'

'I can see what I have said to you displeases you and you are not happy to seek the real God.'

'I can do no more for you except wish you well with God's blessing.'

James stood up and, in a bewildered state, shook John's hand and was escorted to the entrance of the building and from there made his way home.

CHAPTER 6

James returned home in somewhat of a daze state and went straight up to his study and sat in his chair thinking what had transpired with John Bishop. His mind was a blank and he could not concentrate on the main points discussed. He stayed there for an hour without making a noise.

His wife Sue was out shopping when James came home and therefore, she did not know he was home when she returned from the shops. She parked her car and carried in the shopping and unpacked everything, placing the meat and vegetables in the fridge. The study door was closed when she went upstairs and wondered why? She opened the door and was confronted with the spectacle of her husband dangling from a rope with one end tied to a rafter in his study and the other end of the rope around her husband's throat.

She immediately screamed and did not believe what she saw. Sue looked for a knife or a pair of scissors to cut her husband down but could find anything at hand. She ran into the kitchen and grabbed a knife and ran upstairs to the study. The kids who were in the kitchen getting a drink, seeing her in a stressful state, ran after her.

Sue ran into the study and started cutting the rope around her husband's throat. The kids ran into the study and froze, seeing their father dangling in the air. Swinging from side to side as Sue tried to cut the robe.

Sue screamed out to her son to call the ambulance, and he immediately ran downstairs and made the call to triple one. Sue finally cut the rope and her husband fell to the floor, hitting the chair beneath him, forcing it to turn on its side.

He was motionless, and she loosened the noose around his neck and began giving him mouth to mouth resuscitation. He was not responding, so she began pushing on his chest while he laid there. Still no response. She again gave him mouth to mouth resuscitation, but still no response. By that time, the ambulance had arrived and was let in by her son, who was waiting at the front door and led the way.

The paramedics, upon entering the room, could see the rope around the neck of the body and realised it was a suicide attempt. One of them immediately grabbed the defibrillator unit and placed the pads on James's chest and released a charge which shook James's body, lifting it up from the floor. The other paramedic came over to the opposite side and placed his stethoscope on James's chest, trying to hear a heartbeat, but there were none. He said 'No pulse or heat beat. Try again.'

The first paramedic placed the pads again on James's chest and pressed the button. Again, a charge went through James's body, shaking it off the floor. They again tried to see if there was a pulse and a heartbeat, but nothing.

First Paramedic said, 'I am sorry he is not responding, and we can do no more for him. It seems he had passed before we arrived. We will have to notify the police of the situation. Please leave things as they are until the police arrive.'

Sue was beside herself and could not hold her emotions any longer and burst into tears before collapsing near James's body.

The paramedics lifted her up and placed her in a chair and took a bottle of smelling salts from his bag and placed it under her nose, which immediately forced her to regain consciousness.

Her two children, seeing what had happened, ran to her side and were in tears thinking she also had died screaming "Mummy, mummy!!".

Sue got up off the chair and, while still sobbing, took the children into the lounge room and told them to stay there. She immediately phoned a friend and briefly advised her the James had committed suicide and asked her to come over and help her with the children while she manages the arduous task of being interviewed by the police. Sue then went back into the study and sat down in the chair, staring at James's body.

The paramedics had phoned the police.

Sue's friend Jane arrived with her husband and rang the front doorbell.

Sue went downstairs and opened the door and upon seeing Jane with her husband again burst into tears, while holding her head down as if she was going to pass out again.

Jan and her husband Allan ran to her side and held her up and took her into the lounge room and sat her down in the chair. She got up immediately and hugged her friend Jane, crying while hugging her.

After a minute, they calmed her down just as a paramedic came up to Sue and advised her they were going to give her a mild sedative and she agreed to it. He had in his hand a needle already prepared and injected this into her upper arm. After a few minutes, she calmed down and sat crying into some tissue which were handed to her by Jane. The children looked on and were terribly upset themselves in witnessing all that had happened.

Jane and her husband both left Sue and went into the study and saw James lying on the floor where he fell. They could see the robe around his neck. They stood there for a moment and walked out briskly back to where Sue was sitting.

The doorbell rang, and Jane went to the door. The police introduce themselves and were shown in by Jane. She took them into the lounge room and advised Sue of their presence.

The paramedics took the police aside and advised them of the situation and gave them a complete report when they arrived and what transpired afterwards. The police then went into the study and examined James's body lying on the floor. After a few minutes, they took the paramedics' details and went back to the lounge room where Sue was sitting, still in a stressful state and shaking with grief and nerves. The police could see Sue was not in a condition to give them a statement, nor could she look after the children.

The police, after speaking with Jane, agreed that she would take the children with her back to her place and look after them for a few days while the paramedics would transport Sue to the hospital for observation. The police would arrange for James's body to be transferred to the city morgue, where an autopsy would ensure no foul play had occurred.

Sue agreed and went over to the children, telling them they would go to Jane's house for a few days, and she would come and collect them soon. She kissed each of them and then went with the paramedics to the ambulance and was transported to the hospital.

Jane and Allan went to the children's rooms and took out some clothes and underwear they would need for a few days' stay over. Allan went into the kitchen and found some garbage bags and they placed the clothes inside these.

Shortly after Sue left, another police van arrived. Two men come inside the house with a body bag and photographic equipment. They photographed the room and the body and placed the body into the body bag and carried the body out and placed it in the van. After a few minutes of talk with the other police, they drove off and headed for the morgue.

The police took Jane and Allan's details and left for their next call.

Jane and Allan took the children into the car and strapped them in. Jane stayed in the car with the children while Allan went back and locked up and made sure all taps were off and blinds closed. He then locked the front door and got in the car and Jane drove off.

CHAPTER 7

Two days later, Sue laid in bed heavily sedated and trying to remember what had happened and wondered why her husband had not come to visit her. She stared at the ceiling, looking into nothing with her brain, was trying to think things out, but it could not and all she could do was stare into a black hole.

John Bishop was making his weekly visits to the hospital wards, asking people if they needed help or wished help to pray to God. For the last three years, he had been doing this as a community service and knew his way around the hospital.

He was visiting his last ward when a nurse pulled him aside and advised him of Sue Chu's situation and condition. He remembered a Mr Chu saw him a few weeks previously, a James Chu, and he wondered whether Sue was James's wife. The nurse did not mention James's name, just continually referring to her husband.

John asked the nurse to check the name of her husband and a few minutes later she came back and advised him it was Janes Chu who had suicided.

Many thoughts went through John's mind at that moment whether he caused James to take his own life by advising him on the day he suicided he could not help him. Maybe if he took more time with James, he would still be alive.

John recalled James said that his wife and children used to go to church but ceased to go after the Chinese killed their parents.

He walked up to her bed and could see she was distraught. He tried to speak to her, but she still stared at the ceiling into nothing, not even blinking, not acknowledging his presence. He sat on the side of the bed and took her hand and prayed to the Lord to help her through this difficult period. After finishing his pray he left, intending to come back the next day to see if he could speak with her.

The police investigating James's suicide checked his movement on the day of his death and noted he had an appointment with John Bishop. They drove to St John's church and asked to see the bishop. They were shown to John's office and shortly later, John Bishop walked in and introduced himself.

Fist Officer said, 'Bishop, we understand you met with James Chu on the day of his suicide. Can you tell us about what was said?'

John replied, 'Sorry, my surname is Bishop. I am not a Bishop just a minister. I am sorry, but I cannot tell you about James Chu but recommend you speak to his psychiatrist, Dr Hyneman. I met James on that day, and we spoke about his depression and what causes depression. I advised him that the causes of depression were medical causes, body chemistry, or an ill or torched soul. He advised me he did not believe in God and since that was his situation, I advised him I could not help him, and he would have to rely on Dr Hyneman for treatment as what I would say to him would not have any meaning or effect on him as it seemed he was suffering from a psychiatric condition and not a torched soul. He left shortly afterwards, and I never heard from him again.'

First Officer said, 'Did you try to find out why he did not believe in Jesus Christ?'

John replied, 'Yes but unfortunately, I cannot discuss this with you unless you get a warrant. Otherwise, I would be in breach of the privacy act. If this is a private enquiry officer, you can make an appointment and we can discuss your personal situation. Many are in the same position as you and want to know more about Jesus Christ and the real purpose you have been placed on this earth. Give it some thought and give me a ring if you want to discuss this further.'

The police stood up and John escorted them to the entrance of his office and, after shaking hands, they left.

John went back into his office and sat back, wondering if he could have handled the situation better, especially knowing that depression causes people to lose hope. He thought, was James's condition a mental problem or a tormented soul?

John's secretary stood at the door and advised him other parishioners were waiting to see him, who had appointments and that he was running behind time.

He went to the waiting room and invited the next group, who were waiting for him, into his office. This routine went on for the rest of the morning when he stopped for a sandwich and then resumed his busy schedule until four o'clock.

When he had completed his day's work, he drove to the hospital to see how Sue Chu was doing. He walked to her ward. She was sitting up in bed, seemingly much improved from the previous day.

As he approached her bed, Sue woke up and he could see that she did not know who he was.

John said, 'My name is John Bishop. I am the minister at St John's church and look after religious maters in the hospital. How do you feel?'

Sue replied, 'Not too good, but improving.'

John said, 'Your husband came to see me on the day he suicided and told me you are a christian but recently have decided not to continue with your faith, because of what had happened to your parents at the hands of the Chinese.'

Sue said, 'I am not sure why he came to you because he was being treated by Dr Hyneman for depression.'

John said, 'Sue I know that you have a lot going through your mind at present but when you get out of hospital and need to speak to someone about your faith, then please come and see me so we can discuss what is preventing you from reaching out and again connecting with God. I will leave my card with you, so you have my details.'

John left Sue and drove back to his office. He sat at his desk there thinking, will she contact me?

CHAPTER 8

They released Sue from the hospital two weeks after she was admitted. The children stayed with Jane and Allan for a further few days, giving Sue time to settle in.

After a further week, Sue went back to work. She was supported by her employer and could juggle her hours around to suit her needs.

After a few months, Sue noticed she was continually unhappy and not feeling well. She went to her family doctor who, after examining her, began treating her for depression. The doctor concluded that her condition was because of James's absence and the immediate need to attend his funeral after leaving the hospital.

The coroner's report declared there was no foul play involved, and that James suicided while being depressed, which in his belief was brought on by feeling guilty about the cause of his family's death.

Sue was placed on medication for her depression, but there still seemed as if something was wrong, and she could not think things out. She would come around after looking at a blank wall for quite some time.

She was going through her papers one day and came across John Bishop's card. After thinking about it for several days, she made an appointment to see him, hoping to discuss her situation with the minister.

She made the appointment and attended John's office on the day. John said, 'Sue, it is good to see you. How can I help you?'

Sue replied, 'My depression is getting worse, and I am finding myself more often or not just staring into a deep black hole. I was intending to come back to church but still believe God does not care about me or the children. My upbringing tells me this is not the case and I often have visions of my parents when staring into nothing, telling me to seek God. I am of no use to the children in my present state as I cannot be with them too long as I lose my temper or switch off and do not care what they are saying. I have spoken to Dr Hyneman who has placed me on some trial medication, which helps sometimes, but he believes my problem is not psychiatric or chemistry, but my inner self, my soul.'

John said, 'Sue, you have no one that can help you and you gave up the only one who could help you. Your problem is the same as James's except you were a christian and believed in God and over time lost focus of reality. You were placed on this earth to serve God and not the other way around. What you said to Jesus was do it my way or you're nothing to me. Ideology set in and you worshipped self and believed you were capable of all things, which we know is not the case.'

'You know the Pharisee tried to trap Jesus by raising a question which was meant to cause an uprising. They asked should a person pay taxes or should that money be used for a better cause such as for humanity.'

'Jesus asked for a coin and then asked whose inscription or face was on the coin. The Pharisee answered the question and Jesus declared, 'Give unto Caesar that which belongs to Caesar, and charity to the poor.'

John asked, 'What did he mean by what he said?'

Sue replied, 'Give to the poor what you can, I assume.'

John said, 'No, not quite. What he meant is you should have faith in God and in his creation. He created the world and the Chinese Government and not the other way around. He runs the world and not the Chinese Government. Give them what is rightfully theirs and help the poor whenever needed.'

'What you did with protesting in Hong Kong is to say we do not believe God will establish democracy in Hong Kong, so we will take matters into our own hands and do it ourselves. You would not trust in God, nor were you willing to hand over to the Chinese what was rightfully theirs. The demonstrators decided that all of you together were far greater than God on His own, which was the basis of the riots and protests. By all means. You can protest in an orderly way, and still hold faith in God. But in Hong Kong, the protesters decided the reinstatement of democratic rights was to be by their hands and no one was willing to leave it to God, to do what was right as this could have conflicted with their intentions.'

'The mob did not care what God had planned or what he wanted. It was what they wanted, and that was all that counted to them. No one had faith in God nor cared about His plan.'

'What you ended up with is anarchy and the Chinese Government resuming control by military force. The world could not prevent it as the country belonged to China, and they had the legitimate right to step in and unarm the mob, and that is exactly what they did.'

'There is little doubt they took matters further than just taking control. They killed the innocent in the process which your parents were amongst these. They were innocent bystanders to a conflict started by yourselves.'

You failed in your trial, Sue, because you had no faith in God and followed your husband, who was not a christian as this was the popular course of action. Your faith was disposable. James knew of God but had no belief, whereas you knew God but gave Him no consideration. You supported your husband and allowed him and other protest members to make the big decision, which now has led to innocent lives being lost.

'Self-control is a benefit given to the Holy Spirit (Galatians 5:23) and is something we should not pass over to another person or spirit. There was no self-control during the protests.'

'Those things outside our control are safely in the Craftsman's hands, shaping and moulding us into what He would have us be. The Lord knew you had abandoned Him and left you to your own devices, which has led to China taking control of Hong Kong and the death of your parents.'

'Where from here?'

'As stated, these things just did not happen. God knew what was to be the outcome of your violent demonstrations. God has a plan, and He used the demonstrations and occupation of Hong Kong to show what happens when humanity takes matters into their own hands and decides they know better than God. We do not know his plan but can only say,' 'Lord, I have sinned by taking matters into my own hands, and now pass this to you to handle. I have total faith in you and know you will do a better job than what I could do.'

'We come under stress when our commitments are greater than our ability or energy to fulfill them. Overworked, lack of work, inability to put food on the table or pay bills, loss of self- control, aging, financial problems all lead to a guilty feeling and stress. Some of these things are outside of our control.'

'Destructive stress occurs when we find ourselves in a position where our commitments are greater than our ability or energy to fulfill them. It is as if everyone else runs our lives but ourselves. Much of this can be our own fault, as we cannot speak the truth or say no to requests, for fear of the consequences.'

'Emotional stress brought about from grief is the main stress point that takes us closest to depression. Bereavement is a road that must be travelled and could lead to depression, loss of confidence and self-worth.'

'The bible teaches us that in the world we will have tribulations, and we are to expect them. Some being greater than others.'

'A common cause of depression is an inappropriate reaction to events. We know this as "reactive depression" and describe depression without an underlying cause.'

'Depression takes hold of us when we are reacting inappropriately to the events of our lives. When depressed, one cannot feel God's grace but may remember it. Remind yourself of God's redemption and the memory of that redemption past and future will carry you through the times when you cannot feel His presence.'

'Survival is not how we feel but what we remember what God did for us and continually does for us.'

John says, 'It is not to say that you will not get depressed if you have faith in God. Yes, you may be tested to see if you truly have faith in God. If things do not go your way, then pray to the Lord, acknowledging that things seem to have gone contrary to your intentions and that you recognise He is in control. Acknowledge He is the creator, and all things are possible unto Him. Tell the Lord that while you are not happy and able to understand what and why things are occurring, you accept he is in control and allow Him to show you when he is ready, why these things are happening and their purpose. Leave it to God and have faith in Him, for He created the world and mankind.'

Sue says, 'Yes I guess you're right.'

John says, 'Sue, you must decide whether you wish to have a relationship with God on his terms. Because if it is on your terms, then there will be no relationship. If you want to carry God around in your back pocket and take Him out whenever its suites, then be honest with yourself. You have the intentions of appointing yourself as God and not Jesus Christ. In these instances, you believe you are greater than Him and can do a better job than He can. You have adopted ideology and have discarded Jesus Christ. This situation will exist until your circumstances change to bring you back to realise you have been fooling yourself and you are no match for Him. Remember, it may be too late for you, and you die in sin, not believing or relying on Jesus to ensure you have an internal life.'

'Sue, the ball is in your court. Go home and think about what we have discussed and decide what you want to do. I will pray for you, asking the Lord to help you reunite with him and have the Holy Spirit guide you back to having faith in Jesus Christ.'

'If you feel you are not ready, then leave it until you are.'

'If you decide no, I do not believe in Jesus Christ, then go your own way and live the life you want to, rather than the life He has planned for you.'

'No matter what you decide, keep seeing Dr Hyneman and keep taking your medication.'

'Remember what we discussed that three things bring on depression. A medical condition of the mind, a chemistry condition of the body, or a disturbed and upset soul. In your case, the situation is pointing to a disturbed soul and, like it or not, you address this now or carry the burden for the rest of your life.'

'Ring me if you want to discuss the matter further.'

With that, John stared momentarily at Sue, who looked at John with eyes wide open and a blank, pale look on her face.

Both rose from their chairs and John escorted Sue to the door, and she went out to her car, and drove home.

CHAPTER 9

It was one in the morning and Sue woke up abruptly, thinking someone was in her room. She stared in the dark and through the light shining from the streetlight into her room to see if a burglar had entered her bedroom to steal from her.

She could see nothing, no one there, just a light breeze blowing the curtains.

It dawned upon her she had a dream in which she was speaking to her parents who were telling her not to blame herself for their death. That there was a purpose which will be revealed to her in time.

She got out of bed and stared out the window, thinking it was her mind playing a joke on her. It was her fault as she, along with others, wanted democracy for Hong Kong and she did not care what Jesus wanted or what He had in mind. It was what the demonstrators wanted.

James suicided, as he could not face the reality that there was a price to pay for democracy and an injured soul was part of the price. He believed he caused his parent's death and if he refrained from protesting that they would still be alive. He would not accept that we cannot predict the future and that it was the Chinese Government alone who was responsible for the death of his family. It was on their orders that they were shot and killed. Not the natural order of society or humanity. Yes, the demonstrators took matters into their own hands rather than relying on God, but when has God done anything at the request of humanity? You ask, but rarely is help given, and you don't get a reply to your prays.

Sue intended to forget about God and what John had said, and to continue living her own life and making all her own decisions. She went back to bed and eventually dozed off. She woke again with the alarm ring at six and went to wake her children and get them ready for school.

She got the kids up and into the kitchen for breakfast and then into the bathroom for a shower and dressed for school. She had breakfast with the kids and then showered.

Once everyone was ready, she bundled them into the car and drove off towards the school. The kids were dropped off and she went off to work.

At work, she received a telephone call from her boss, who wanted to see her immediately. She got up and walked to his office, where other solicitors had gathered.

Partner says, 'I have asked you all here to advise you we have been chosen to prepare an application to take China to the International Human Rights Commission, in their handling of the demonstrators in Hong Kong and mainland China, and the killing of relatives of those who took part in the demonstrations. I am glad to say we have been chosen not only to make a case against them but also to litigate this matter.'

'Additional to the expertise we have in this area; we have several lawyers who were directly involved in the demonstrations and who also lost parents on mainland China. They have firsthand knowledge of what took place. While we urge you not to treat this as a personal application, but one on humanitarian grounds. The Chinese Government will resist the application who will no doubt deny the killings or that they were unlawful. We must get evidence to support our case, which will not be easy as the Government of China will ensure that no one in that country helps us otherwise, they will end up in prison or dead.'

'Those lawyers who have firsthand experiences and who have been affected by the brutality of the Chinese can ask to be excused from being part of the team. We will have the responsibility to prepare the application and litigate the case. The memories of relatives being killed in China may be too much for you, plus the threat that China will retaliate against your families who still live in mainland China may cause you to decline being part of this team. However, those who have lost their family in China might want to be part of the team. In these instances, the Chinese Government cannot threaten our application by putting pressure on your relatives, as now none exist.'

'We want you all to think about the assignment and if invited to join the team, whether you will do so? The partner in charge of the project is Jeremiah Cummins. He prefers to be called Jerry, and he will be on the tenth floor. Thank you for attending today's meeting and we will now break up and allow you to get back to work.'

The meeting broke up and everyone went back to their desks and to work.

Sue specialised in Human Rights, Discrimination and International Law and had completed several cases since commencing work at the law firm. The firm recognised her as an astute lawyer, and she was a member of the American Bar Association and was qualified to practice in Australia. She wondered if she would be considered, but dismissed the thought as she was relatively new to the firm and possibly other lawyers would be asked to join instead of her.

She completed her work midweek when she received a call from Jerry Cummins asking her to come to his office. She took the lift to the tenth floor and then walked to his office, where he was waiting for her. They went into his office and sat down.

Jerry said, 'Sue, I understand you came from Hong Kong and were involved in the demonstrations there for democracy.'

Sue replied, 'Yes, both me and my husband were involved.'

Jerry said, 'Your husband was a doctor, wasn't he?'

Sue replied, 'Yes, before he suicided.'

Jerry said, 'Suicided. Why did he do that after escaping from the Chinese?'

Sue replied, 'In his mind we failed in our mission in that the Chinese arrested all those involved in the protests and killed all their parents and relatives who lived in China. His father warned him of what would happen, but he would not listen to him. He blamed himself for their death rather than blaming the Chinese Government.

If he dropped his involvement, they most probably would still be alive. He would have been arrested and sent to jail, but they would still be alive. He couldn't accept their death was at the hands of the Chinese Government and took his own life after a bout of depression.'

Jerry said, 'I am sorry to hear of your pain. Possibly, this will only stir up memories for you and affect the quality of your work. We should overlook you at present and use you down the track.'

Jerry said, 'What about your own situation? Do you have bouts of depression?'

Sue replied, 'Yes, but I am taking medication, and it is under control.'

Jerry says, 'That's good to know, but what about your soul? Depression in these instances comes from a tormented sole rather than tormented brain.'

Sue replied, 'I have spoken to a minister, but find it hard to regain a relationship with God. I prefer to do things my way rather than rely on a spirit that no one can see or speak to.'

Jerry says, 'What you are telling me is that you have lost the faith you once had.'

Sue says, 'Yes. It seems for good.'

Jerry says, 'Well, if you feel you are up to it, I can use you, so I will make an office available for you on this floor and you can join me at the commencement of the new week. If that is all right?'

Sue replies, 'Yes thank you. I am sure this assignment will be challenging.'

Both stood up and Jerry escorted Sue to the door, and she went back to her office to finish her work.

CHAPTER 10

The newspapers and press were having a field day in China, declaring China would suspend the trade of coal and other raw materials being shipped from Australia. It declared it was forced to make such a radical decision based on "irregularities in paperwork". Ships on route from Australia to China would not be allowed to disembark at Chinese ports.

Australian Government attempted to resolve the situation personally by telephoning their counterpart in China without success. The Chines Government nor any of their ministers were prepared to front up and declare the suspension to trade with Australia was a political decision and had nothing to do with paperwork.

This embargo was the first of many that were forced onto Australia in retaliation of them refusing to co-operate with Beijing on human rights issues and on Australia insisting on the investigation of the source of the COVID-19 pandemic, which they believed came out of Wuhan China.

Agricultural crops such as barley were refused entry into China with the view of crippling the Australian economy, forcing the government to do a backflip and toe the line as dictated by Beijing.

The Australian Government recognising what Beijing was doing and exhausted all avenues to bring the matter to mediation, but the

Chinese Government made it clear it was not willing to open its markets to Australia even though China had recently negotiated and signed a trade agreement with Australia.

China imposed tariffs on wine and other goods, making Australian goods prohibitive to purchase in China. False propaganda followed China's action, declaring lies about Australia and discrediting the country as a tourist destination.

The Australian Government, not wishing to confront the Chines, took a weak, passive approach towards China and refused to listen to its own parliamentary ministers who were advocating the confiscation of all assets acquired by China in Australia and a more aggressive approach to China on future trade agreements.

The Australian Government began proceedings against China in the World Trade Organisation, filling an application of unethical behaviour by China towards Australia in matters of trade.

The Chinese Government did not care about the actions brought against them as they knew it would be years before these matters would be heard and by then they assume the Australian economy would be crippled.

Australia, realising China was not a friend, began the long road to finding new markets for its produce and products. It would never again trust China to keep its word or act ethically in matters of trade.

China showed that while it demanded respect, it lacked honesty and credibility and will lie to get its way.

China gained its produce from other countries even though these were not of the same quality and were dearer than the Australian products.

America under Trump had made it clear four years ago that America would not be the world cop and would look after its own back yard only. China flexed its muscles, its might and through its aggression, gained positions both economically and strategically in Africa and the Asian/Pacific region.

Other countries in Europe and America argued, Australia should adopt a world leading law to apply targeted sanctions on human right abuse by China.

The Law Council of Australia had welcomed the recommendations in the Parliament's human right subcommittee's final report to adopt a law like the US Magnitsky Act to address human rights violations and corruption.

The Chinese Government took any negative report about Australia and blew it out of all proportion and exaggerated the truth to ensure the population in China understood why the Government refused to trade with Australia. The Chinese population only accepted these lies for a short time, as they knew what their government was capable of.

The Australian Government, however, continually looked weak in accepting the lies spread by the Chinese and trade sanctions imposed by them. They refused to act aggressively to show Beijing that they would not be pushed around and stand idly by while its economy was being crippled. They refused to restrict the sale of iron ore to China as a lever to get China back to the negotiating table or to honour their commitments under the free trade agreement that the Chinese broke.

The Government some time ago agreed to allow one of its major ports to be leased to the Chines on a ninety-nine-year arrangement. This was a strategic port to the north of the country where military vessels and commercial ones arrived for trade and military manoeuvres. The Chinese, therefore, controlled the in and out movements in the port, including container shipping.

Certain Ministers urged the Government to begin proceedings on national grounds to take back the port. This would show China that it would not just be all their way and that there were things that could be done should they act as "mongrels". However, the Government lacked the courage to take China on and took the soft approach, hoping they would see reason.

Australia also refused to place tariffs on goods coming from China into Australia even though China had placed a tariff of three hundred percent on Australian Goods entering China, which directly violated the free trade agreement between the two countries.

Other countries in Europe and America made representations to the Chinese but always stopped short of threatening the Chines

Government with sanctions or tariffs should they continue their unfair dealing against Australia.

China looked like the Nazis in Germany in the nineteen forties, where they were left to do whatever they wanted to do as long as they left other countries alone.

China established a naval port in the South Pacific and was challenged, but the port remains and is increasing in size by the day. It laughs at the representation's nations make at the United Nations as it knows that these will lead to nothing. It has moved into the vacuum America created when it removed itself from acting as the world's police officer.

China's economy has grown substantially even during the pandemic crises, and while it still declares itself as a developing nation, it is recognised as the second largest economy to that of America.

Human rights are not a problem in China, especially when the Government acts to remedy the situation rather than worrying about due process. It has no concern for dissident and jails all troublemakers, without concern for their rights. The courts are dictated to by the Government and do not apply the Rule of Law as in democratic countries. Freedom of speech is also not a problem as the Government controls what is to be printed and broadcasted on television. If you get exposure and criticise the Communist Party or Government, you will be hauled off to prison or killed while trying to escape. Corruption is bound in China, and you have not only to worry about your own survival but also that of any relatives or family members still living in China. If you step out of line, then all your family pays the price. This is to show to others what will happen to them if you act against the Communist Party.

The Chinese will not allow freedom of religion and currently have gathered one million Muslims for re-education and training. They are being taught the fallacy of their religion and will come out of the camp accepting they are no longer followers of Muhammad.

The Chinese Government has done this with limited exposure and no Muslim country has protested or demanded investigation of the matter nor has it yet been brought before the International Human Rights Commission.

Other religions have been dealt with similarly and China has declared it does not need God. The Government has taken this position and will deal ruthlessly with anyone trying to reintroduce religion into the country. The State dictates if religion or worship is allowed and to what extent.

CHAPTER 11

I n the hills in the Eastern Province lies a small church run by a
monk and two helpers. The monk is named Lim Bow. Most of
the villagers in Chan Low are Christians and believe in Jesus
Christ, and the village has always had a belief in and followed the
teachings of the Bible.

The monk prays constantly at the church for his villagers and the
prosperity of the village is seen by the health of the people and the
land. The crop ratio from the province far exceeds those of other areas
of China and the village has come to the attention of the Government
in Beijing. The National People's Committee, the ruling committees
in China, has declared that the church is practising black-magic and
therefore, by using this to their advantage, can produce more and
better-quality produce.

The government does not accept their explanation as to why they
can achieve a greater yield per acre and has agreed to send a delegation of
three with an escort to the province to find out what is happening there.

They make their way to the village by helicopter with enough
men to surround the outskirts of the village. The delegation insists
on meeting with the People's Committee, which gathers as a group
upon hearing the helicopters.

After the pleasantries, they all sit in the common building, and
the delegation is offered tea and some biscuits.

The delegation is introduced to the People's Committee, and the purpose of their arrival is stated. They are advised that all in their village believe in a christian God, and most people pray daily to the Lord.

The delegation advised the Committee that this must stop as the Government will not allow religion in China and will insist on the church being demolished. The Government has taken over all religions and should be respected as being 'God of The People' and there is to be no worship of any other God other than the Communist Party. The committee advised that they would have to speak with the monk and see what he had to say. They arranged a meeting for the next day.

The head of the People's Committee is an elderly man in his seventies, who had a lean from the waste from spending his youth in the fields attending to his crops. He could not straighten up and always looked humble. He could not read or write Chinese. His name was Mane Chow, and he was well respected by all in the village.

The People's Committee gathered in the church and the ultimatum that was given was conveyed to the monk, who became disturbed by what he heard. After some discussion, they agreed they would meet at the town centre where all that wanted could attend and hear what was being said.

The People's Committee members were present as was the monk and after about ten minutes the three government delegates arrived with their military escort and momentarily stood there, then one of them stepped forward and said "The National People's Congress (NPC) has declared it would not allow a religion of any type in China, and all religions are to cease immediately. All religious practices such as christening and baptising are also to cease immediately. The NPC has made laws in this regard and as to ethics, abortions, euthanasia, and you are to follow these laws and not any religious doctrine. We have orders to arrest those who oppose the will of the people and to bring them back to Beijing for trial. We also have been directed to find out why your province is prospering and producing a greater volume of crops than any other. What is your secret? Is it some fertiliser or special chemicals used to grow your crops? You must tell us, or we will arrest your committee members and take them with us for interrogation. Who of you is the head of the committee?"

Mane Chow steps forward but is frozen by fear and stands trembling in front of the delegation. The monk, fearing they might shoot Mane Chow, steps forward and says, 'The National People's Congress has made a golden calf in creating the Central Committee of six. They have changed the laws of the land to suit their agenda and now have done away with the creator, our God. This land is not yours, but Gods and he will do what he decides and not, as you or your congress decide. You may destroy the building, but you will never destroy God's church. You threaten the Lord and have made laws outlawing worship of the Lord. Deciding to replace His word with Laws, which are made by men and are changed to suit their agendas.'

The spokesperson for the delegation said, 'Arrest them. They refuse the follow our laws. We will take them to Beijing for questioning and allow The National People's Congress to decide their fate.'

The guards immediately took the monk and the three committee members. While others telephoned for support. After about twenty minutes, three additional helicopters arrived, and they took those arrested on board and all took off for Beijing.

Upon arriving at the capital, they were immediately taken to a detention centre and placed in a cell to await their fate.

They were forced to stay in detention for two days and were then brought before The National People's Congress for questioning.

The full assembly was present.

The President stood up and said, 'We have been advised that you refuse to accept our decision to do away with all religions and to advise us of how your province has become so prosperous and achieve the yield it does. Surely, we are not asking too much from you?'

The monk steps forward and begins speaking, 'We are all overwhelmed by what has happened to us and that we have been brought before this great assembly. Our secret is not a secret. It is simple and known by all in our village. To get to the answer did not require a contingent of militia however, it requires acceptance of the truth. We believe in Jesus Christ our Lord and pray for his mercy and blessing. It is He who provides the clean air and abundance of rain and sunshine so we can grow our crops. The environment provided keeps our people healthy and free from pandemics and diseases. This is our secret, but to duplicate it, stop your attack on religion and allow the people's free choice of worship. In God's eyes, you have become the poor substitute for Him, and he will punish you unless you change your ways.'

'God gives His treasure to all that believe in Him.'

President stands and says, 'We control this country, not God. It will be as we direct and not by his command.'

Monk replies, 'You have spilt innocent blood here in China and Hong Kong without concern or regret and for this the Lord will condemn you and your congress.'

President says, 'It will be us who condemn you all. You will be put on trial for treason. We will order the destruction of your church and your families will join you in prison.'

Monk says, 'Let it be known that the Lord will not allow one brick to fall from the church, let alone for it to be destroyed. As for your praises for yourself and refusing to allow credit to go to God, the Lord will turn his face from China, and it will no longer have his support. You will learn what it is to live without God. Swarms of locusts will infest your fields and your crops will be subject to disease. Diseases which will kill many of the country's people. God will not hear your cries of mercy nor come to your aid. Those that support the Congress will learn a bitter lesson and see that God created mankind and not the other way around and what it means to live without God.'

President says, 'We do not need your God. We can do all things ourselves and do not rely on a magician. Get them out of the assembly and have them tried by the court. We look for a life sentence for them and their families.'

The men who had committed no crime were taken out and placed back in jail, waiting for their trial. The Committee who rules the country can dictate the sentence they are relying from the court. There is no Rule of Law in China. The people in China think the Court is independent, but it is not. It follows the will of the government. Judges there do as dictated by the State, or they are replaced with others who will do as instructed.

The President says, 'I put to the Congress a motion that the men brought before us be tried in court and we seek life sentence for them and their families, for treason. That the church they spoke of in the village be destroyed, its people be made to confess their practices or face a lifetime in jail. Those that agree raise your hands.'

No one had their hands down. All raised upright to ensure they were not pointed out and made an example of.

President says, 'The proposal was unanimously carried. Let it be implemented as an order of The National People's Congress.'

The men were taken out and put back into their cell.

About two hours later, the President came down to the prison to ensure the men were there and not let out.

He spoke to the guards, advising them that these men have been convicted and all that is delaying their execution is the Court Order. He advised them that the men are to be shot as soon as this is sent to the prison.

The guard thinks about the men and decides not to worry about feeding them as they were to be shot and he could pocket the money rather than spend it on meals. He locks up the jail and goes off home, leaving the prisoners in jail.

CHAPTER 12

The men are hungry and find it hard to sleep on an empty stomach. No one falls asleep but drift off and wake up after twenty minutes.

Around midnight, the men are awakened by the image of a man in black moving around the police station. The man opens a draw and takes out a set of keys and approaches the Jail. He hesitates for a moment and comes close to the bars of their cell.

The man says, 'Your prays have been heard and the Lord shall release you. You are to make your way up the street quietly and locate four motor bikes parked in the car park nearby. One bike has chicken and rice in a bag hanging off the handlebars. Drive off home and after driving an hour park your bikes and part take in the food. There are two bottles of water also hanging off the handlebars, with some chocolate bars in the bag.

The men try to look at the face of the man speaking but could not see his features. The monk asks, 'Who are you?'.

The man on the other side said, 'I am the angle of the Lord.' With that the man unlocked the cell and vanished in the darkness.

The men opened the cell door and went out and moved to the front door. They opened the door and walked out onto the street. They walked up the street until they stood opposite to a car park that was full of military trucks. They look around and found the four bikes behind some parked trucks. They notice a man in uniform moving around the bikes and he placed bags on both sides of one of the bikes. He then steps away and walks up the street towards some shops and enters one of the noodle shops.

Not wanting to be caught, the prisoners move up to where the bikes are standing and notice that each has a key in the ignition. The Monk sits on the bike with the two bags on the handlebars and starts up the bike. The other men do the same and each drive out of the car park and head towards the Eastern Province.

Ater driving an hour, they pull over behind some thick trees and open the bags on the Monks handlebars. As advised by the angel, there was chicken and rice for them to eat and water for them to drink. They had their fill and wrapped up the leftovers and placed everything in the side storage compartments at the back of the Monk's bike. They washed their hands, went to the toilet behind a tree, and drove off home.

The next morning, the guard came into the station and opened up. He raised the blinds on the windows to let in the light and changed the calendar to the correct date and then moved to the cells to see why things were so quiet. He stared into the cell and then looked away, not realising there was no one inside. As he turned, he suddenly realised that no one was in the cells. He looked back again and checked the cell door, which was locked. There were no prisoners. He panicked and knew that he would be held responsible for the prisoners escaping, which meant that he and his family would be punished if not shot dead.

He tried to think what to do, but could not think of anything. Eventually, he decided that the best course of action would be to burn the place down and declare that the prisoners were trapped and perished in the fire. He ran up the street to one of the army trucks and took a jerry can out full of petrol, and some hand grenades from one of the trucks.

He splashed the petrol around internally and then went back to the truck to get some more petrol. He took a further two large cans full of petrol from the truck and brought them back to the station, placing one to the east wing of the station and the other in a room facing the west. He then took some string he had in his desk draw and tied it to the bars of the cells and strung the other end with some tap onto the door. He attached several hand grenades to the door so when someone opens the door, it would pull the pin out, causing an explosion. He pulled the blinds down, took his things out of his desk draw and locked the front door as if he had not attended work and went home.

At about nine o'clock his boss arrived with the President, who wanted to speak to the Monk about his God. They tried the front door, but it was locked. The Sargent phoned the guard and was informed that the guard had a sore throat and cold symptoms and thought he had Covid-19. The Sargent did not care what he had as the President was here, and he wanted to speak to the prisoners. The guard made it clear he did not want to spread the various but after being ordered by the Sargent to turn up and open the office; he decided he had no choice but to do so.

The guard turned up after about fifteen minutes and everyone moved away from the front door to make sure they didn't catch the virus. The Guard initially handed the keys to the Sargent put he refused to touch them. He then moved to the front door and unlocked it and stood back.

The Sargent ordered him to open the door, but he said he did not want them to get his virus from touching the doorknob. The President ordered him to open the door, which he did and immediately stepped back to allow the other two men to enter the station. As soon as they entered, there was a loud explosion, and the President was blown outside the station onto the street and laid unconscious, not moving at all. The Sargent who entered first was blown up and could not be found. The station was a blaze with the fire taking hold and destroying all three buildings in the complex, including all records that were kept.

Paramedics were called to attend to the President, who upon their arrival was rushed to the nearest hospital and found to have had a broken arm, concussion and burns on his face and chest. The President remained in hospital for a week and was discharged shortly thereafter. The report advised that all men in the cells were consumed by the fire along with the Sargent. The cause of the fire was put down to a gas leak.

The President was glad the Monk was burnt to death, as he would not be a problem in the future. All that the President had to do was arrange for the same to happen to the Monk's God.

CHAPTER 13

The air force scrambled two plans as directed by the National People's Congress to destroy the church in the Eastern Province.

Fully laden with rockets and incendiary bombs, they headed towards the Eastern Province. Twenty minutes out they radio that heavy cloud has been moving in and it was mainly at the lower rather in the upper atmosphere. They requested radar guidance, which was given. They approached their destination and requested confirmation that they were to proceed, as they could see nothing at ground level. They recommended the mission be aborted until the cloud cover lifted. They were told to carry out their mission.

Co-ordinances were given, and Military Command directed them to fire their rockets, which they did, including dropping several incendiary bombs before flying back to their military air base.

Shortly afterwards, reports came in that a village some distance from the Eastern Province was hit by rockets destroying a hospital and killing all its patients. The officer in charge immediately had the men arrested and thrown into a military jail for killing innocent people. The report on television declared that the pilots disobeyed orders and mistakenly bombed a hospital and not a military target. They would be tried and, if found guilty, would be executed.

The military was going to destroy the church and arrest the family members of those who were consumed in the fire a few weeks ago. They devised a plan where three trucks would go in with ten men in each truck and use explosives to destroy the church.

The convoy headed off at the crack of dawn on a twelve-hour journey. It was clear and dry when they set off. After travelling for three hours, they pulled over on the side of the road and allow everyone to get out and stretch their legs, while one man attended to an overheating problem with one of the trucks.

The men walked away from the trucks and gathered for a smoke some distance from the trucks. A soldier was working under the bonnet when suddenly there was a load explosion, and the truck blew up in a ball of flames. The other two trucks, which were parked close to the first, also caught on fire and exploded, leaving all three trucks in a ball of fire and the soldiers crouching down to ensure the bullets that were held in a rear tray and exploding, did not hit them.

After an hour, the fire burned itself out and all men began the long march back to their base.

The person in charge reported the mission had been accomplished, and they killed the families who tried to escape from the trucks. In the fighting, they lost the three trucks. The men were told to support this lie or else they and their families would suffer. They agreed that all would tell the same story if asked.

The report filtered back to the central office and finally was conveyed to the President.

The villagers in Eastern Province maintained their belief in God and prayed at the church daily. The Lord supported them and, as they grew in faith, blessed them.

CHAPTER 14

Adrian Lim gave his wife and firstborn a kiss before stepping on board his boat. He was a fisherman, and like others, relied on the sea for a living.

The course for the day was to head off the Philippine coast, someone hundred miles from shore, to catch the best fish. He has tried all week to make a catch but on each occasion was prevented from doing so by the Chinese navy who had sent one of their destroyers and a frigate to disrupt the fishermen's efforts to make a living, as they had for the past decades.

On boards was Adrian's father Cheng Lim, a man in his late seventies, his two brothers and his sister. They were getting desperate as the Chinese claimed several islands off the Philippine coast as belonging to them and had forbid anyone coming within two hundred miles circumference of these islands. The Philippine's government refused to accept China's claim, as the Philippines had always declared ownership of the islands and had fished these waters since creation. They had been turned back by the Chinese navy, who had turned water cannons on them to deter them from dropping their nets.

The flotilla going out today comprised six boats. Normally there would be ten or more, but the other boats had been damaged by the Chines navy shelling them as they tried to reel in their catch. Two boats had been sunk and the other boats were damaged to the degree that they were not seaworthy.

Adrian and the flotilla tried to have the Government provide them with an escort, which they did some months earlier. However, the Chinese navy fired missiles at them, destroying the vessels. The Chinese sailors on board the destroyer opened fire on the men as they jumped overboard while their boat sank. There were only three survivors who were pulled from the sea, and all were in a critical condition, with bullet wounds.

The Philippine's government raised the matter in the United Nations, but China vetoed all the motions raised against them. China ensured that any motions that they could not block in the United Nations against them were also defeated as it would force countries who borrowed money from them to vote in their favour, otherwise their loans would be called up immediately.

China declared it would allow fishing in the disputed waters if the Philippines Government openly declared it recognised China's legitimate claim against Taiwan and the islands in the Philippine Seas. The Philippines government refused to be blackmailed into supporting China and made its position well know.

They approached America and Australia for support as these two counties were active in the Pacific and seamed to refuse to bow down to China's demands. America agreed to see what it could do and insisted on Australia supporting its efforts to stem China's aggression towards the Philippines.

The flotilla headed off an hour before dawn so they could make a catch before they were discovered by the China's navy. The journey took several hours as the fish were some distance out to sea in the main current streams.

They arrived at their destination and the instruments showed the fish were in deeper waters than first thought, requiring each of the vessels to drop its nets with weights and trawl to ensure they got a large catch.

Adrian's vessel was the first in position and began trawling to ensure everyone had an equal opportunity to get the fish they came for. Their instruments showed the fish were in a large block following the currents. They trawled for about half an hour and then brought the net to the surface. As they reeled in the net, the second vessel would begin their run and once it had filled its net, it too would stop and real in its net of fish.

Adrian brought his net to the surface to reveal a massive catch. The crane lifted the net on deck and released the lock with the fish gashing out on deck to be sorted. All helped to sort the fish out into their different category and the catch was dumped into ice storage compartments below deck. Adrian then moved his vessel in position to take his turn again at trawling for his second catch once everyone had been given a turn. All the vessels caught more than the usual quantity of fish and everyone was keen to get a second pass and then go home before the Chinese Navy discovered where they were.

King Neptune was protecting them at this point in time.

Adrian made his second run trawling a little deeper, hoping to get more fish this time. They trawled for a half an hour and then reeled the net in and lift the catch on deck. Again, they released the net's lock, and the fish were dumped on deck to be sorted. Again, all pitched in to sort the catch while Adrian's father steered the vessel to a course that would get them home. They stayed on while the other vessels made their second run. As the second vessel was trawling, they noticed a large vessel on the horizon, and they messaged all the other vessels to get a move on as the Chinese Navy had spotted them.

The second vessel completed its catch and secured the fish below deck. The third vessel had just completed its trawling run and was lifting the net on deck when the Chinese destroyer made a move towards it with its water cannon shooting high pressure of water at the vessel. Adrian could see what would happen if they couldn't secure their catch. The fish would be washed back into the ocean, and they would lose everything.

The Chinese destroyer came close to the fishing boat and opened fire with its water cannons. It hit the vessel with such force that the fishing boat rolled over on its side and began to sink. The men jumped into the ocean to ensure they didn't go down with the boat. As they were floating in the ocean, the Chinese destroyer came near and opened fire on the men to drown them or cause some injury, which would prevent them from floating.

Adrian moved his vessel to protect the men. He made sure that the Chinese would fire their water cannon at his boat and not at the men in the water. The water cannon hit Adrian's vessel with such force that his boat rocked up and down as if it was going to be rolled over.

On the second run, Adrian came from a direction on the opposite side and as the cannon started up again, he drew his rifle and aimed it at the man operating the gun. When he passed the destroyer, he pulled the trigger, and the operator collapsed on the deck of destroyers. No one on the destroyer realising what had happened. All the vessels immediately stopped trawling and secured their catch and readied themselves to make the trip home.

Some boats moved closer to pick up the men in the water and to attend to their injuries. One was barely breathing while the other was unconscious, as he had received a direct hit in the head from the water cannon.

The captain of the destroyer, seeing his man with a shoulder wound, ordered his guns to be loaded, intending to blast the boats out of the water. He gave orders for the guns to be aimed at Adrian's and the second boat and gave the order to fire. The guns roared out, but they had not been set correctly with the shells going over the vessel's bowl. Adrian tried to zigzag to ensure they could not get an accurate bearing on him. As he turned his boat, he noticed there were several vessels heading their way, and these vessels were not flying the Chines flag.

The captain, who had not seen the other vessels on the horizon, gave the order to fire at the fishing boats as they came near to them. This time they aimed their guns on the last two vessels and as they came near, they fired their guns at them, hitting one vessel at the rear of the boat and the other at the front with both boats sustaining major damage.

One vessel, an Australian frigate, came close to the Chinese destroyer and fired a shot over its bowl, causing it to tilt over slightly before stabilizing. The frigate was accompanied by two American and two British destroyers. All were on war manoeuvres and noticed what the Chinese destroyer was intending to do.

They radioed the Chinese destroyer that they believe they were acting illegally, as to cause destruction of the fishing vessels and that they were to move on out of the current area where the vessels were fishing.

The captain of the destroyer refused to move away, so the friendly destroyers came alongside of the fishing vessels to protect them from being fired upon. They aimed their guns at the Chinese destroyer, not knowing what would happen next. They escorted the fishing fleet halfway home and once in safe waters, left them so they could continue with their manoeuvres.

These instants were reported to the Chinese government and made world news. The Chinese declared what was reported were lies and gave a different version of events. They declared that the western destroyers tried to provoke the Chinese destroyer into firing first, and it was the west that was at fault and not the Chinese. This story was shown to be a lie, as the western ships filmed the whole event by use of satellites and could prove the Chinese to be the aggressors.

The Philippines government protested to the Chinese government, who would not accept the correct version of events. They would stick to their fabricated lies. However, the world knew the truth but feared to support the Philippines as they would come under the wrath of China.

The Chinese were keen to take on fishing boats who had no guns or weaponry at all. But when it came to someone of their own size, they would back off unless they had the advantage against their opponents.

The issue as to who owns the islands is still a point of contention, and China still prevents fishing in its territorial waters.

The Chinese President was not pleased with the outcome of the confrontation and wanted answers as to why the fishing boats were not blasted out of the water when they had the chance to do so?

CHAPTER 15

The Australian Government received a notice from the Chinese embassy that Chine would refuse to allow the import of barley from Australia. It declared Australia was dumping its produce in China, preventing local farmers competing on price.

Australia objected to the actions taken by China and declared their excuse had nothing to do with protecting local markets, but China's way of dealing with countries who cause embarrassments to the Government of China or disagreed openly with their policies and challenged them.

China refused to discuss the issue further and ordered its ministers not to have any further dialog with Australia on agriculture. China declared it was reviewing imports of other agricultural products from Australia, such as livestock, crabs and wine. The intention was to shut Australia up from making any further comments about China and its policies and stop Australia openly criticising China on the world stage and in the United Nations.

Australia continuously raised issues regards China's attempt to cripple its economy economically and tried to seek support from European nations who had been treated similarly.

Most countries that were approached gave assurance of support but did little in the way of calling in the Chinese ambassador to convey their displeasure about China's actions. They did not want to be next in line to feel the economic displeasure of China and therefore paid lip service to Australia while making sure they did not give recognition of support to Australia but stood neutral.

The China's extended its embargo of Australian goods further. Industries in Australia that relied on China's markets protested to the Australian Government what Australia was doing and urged the government to cease its confrontational policy with China and to bend at the knee at all costs to ensure they regained their markets. Again, the principles of truth and righteousness went out the window and the dollar became the paramount issue here.

The Australian Government, not wanting to risk further deterioration of relationships, did not respond beyond declaring it would take China to the World Trade Organisation for breach of their free trade agreement.

China did not care about this as it knew the process would take years before the matter got to court and by then the world would have changed. It wanted to show what China would do to countries that oppose it or speak openly which would discredit China on the world stage.

China made it clear that no country could stand neutral. You either support China and its policies or you are against China.

The average Australian thought the Government was being too subtle in its handling of China. The discussions in the pub mainly revolved around a consensus that the Government should turf China out of Darwin port and take back Coby Station, making it clear to China, that if it wanted to ignore trade agreements, then Australia was prepared to overturn or cancel other agreements that were made with the Chinese government.

The average Australian wanted the government to seek alternative markets for its produce, and not to sell to China or have any dealings or reliance on them, as they could not be trusted to honour agreements made. They were considered peasants dressed in Amani suites who could never be trusted to uphold their word.

The Australian Government did nothing exceptional except it took the advice of other countries in that it ceased its rhetoric and stopped its criticism of China.

The Chinese economy relied on one commodity that was in demand worldwide, which was mined and sold by Australia. That was iron ore. Ministers urged the Government to use this as a lever towards China and to act tough when China wanted to refuse to honour its commitments to the free trade agreements. However, the Government refused to limit the sale of this commodity to China and took the view that some trade was better than none.

China declared it was using the iron ore to manufacture steel for building and construction purposes, which was not the case. The raw material was used to build war planes, destroyers, and submarines to ensure China had the biggest military capability in preparatory to war.

CHAPTER 16

The Chinese government declared its provinces were going to have the best harvest of grain in a century and that the economy was on its way to record growth and surplus. The outlook was good for China and the Government took the view that nothing could prevent them having the best year in a century.

The Government had not forgotten about its promise to demolish the church and do away with all religions but was assured by the military that this had been done.

The government had the right approach, and nothing could derail their success. It was assured that its military destroyed the church and accepted that its orders had been carried out and it had killed the families of the men. They were awaiting the Court's decision about the men that were held in custody and subsequently thought of being killed in the fire at the holding cells and felt it unnecessary to hold a trial on a matter that had already been decided upon.

The Chinese Government cancelled orders for barley, wheat and other grain crops as all indications were that it would harvest a bumper crop this year and therefore did not need to purchase supplies from other countries. However, there were some conservatives in the National People's Congress who thought that it may be prudent to still acquire crops from some of the African countries to ensure they held surplus grain stocks. These were not of the high quality that they were accustomed to from Australia, but they will do as China was determined to teach Australia a bitter lesson as to who was the dominate force to content with in the South Pacific Region.

Bad news was not something that the provinces readily declared to Beijing and advised them as a last resort. Those with political power saw bad news as a demonstration of weak leadership or unwillingness to do as Beijing directed. The Government would, in most times, replace the person in charge of the village with another and imprison the former to ensure the truth did not get out to the general population. They would also imprison their family to make sure gossip or information did not get relayed through the grapevine. The government, in these instances, tendered to declare the replacement as a normal progression and that they have promoted the former person in command to another position, giving the impression that all was well or even better than was planned or expected.

The villagers in the Eastern Province noticed that the weather was changing, not what was expected seasonally, but different from what normally transpires. This was not climate change, as some expressed it. For instance, in the middle of summer, they experienced three days of freezing weather, followed by three days of rain. They would then get a heat wave drying out the crops. This in some provinces weakened the plants that were ready to harvest and prevented machinery being used in the fields to harvest the crop.

In other provinces, the heat wave caused dry storms to develop and set the fields on fire through lightning strikes. The dry fields burned furiously and on a broad front which widened as the fire moved ahead, driven by roaring winds from combusting crops. Workers tried to fight the fire but could not, as it moved at a speed not seen before and on a broad front.

The fire did not hesitate to burn through villages and forests as the rains previously had caused foliage on the forest floor to grow in density and this became fuel for a gigantic wall of fire.

Villagers lost all their possessions as they were trying to fight the fire with crude implements that were useful in the past but not against the current combustive wall of flames.

All was consumed in the fire's path.

Villagers tried to make fire breaks to stop the fire, but this had no effect as the ambers from the fires were being carried by the hot winds. The ambers were carried for miles beyond the fire's front, starting new fires which would deplete the force able to fight them as many would leave their posts to go to fight the fire approaching their village.

Most tried to protect their homes, too little avail. Some firefighters lost their lives trying to put the fire out or trying to save their village or their home. The death toll rose to alarming levels and reports sent to Beijing described entire villages being burned out and thousands losing their lives in trying to stop the inferno.

Beijing, when advised, realised this was developing into a catastrophe; ordered the military in to fight the fire.

They deployed men on a wide front to stop the fire, but they achieved little. The fire still moved forward at an alarming rate, engulfing everything in its path refusing to be controlled.

Air tankers were ordered in to fight the fire, but there were not enough of them to do the job.

China asked other countries to assist by lending their water bombers. The poor countries did not have the planes to attend to this type of catastrophe. Countries like Canada, Australia and America declared its bombers were required for domestic outbreaks and therefore could not be lent to China to assist them in their fight.

China took this as an insult and declared it would treat these countries with the contempt as they had openly shown that they were not friends of China and were not willing to assist in times of emergency.

China's television reported on the huge fire front and declared that the Government had called out the military to get the fire under control. However, it refused to publicise the number of lives lost and that the fire would affect the country's production.

The air force was ordered to bomb fire breaks ahead of the fire and used incendiary bombs to set the forest alight. Bombs were used to make a path half a mile wide and fifty miles long down a forest path, and rockets were used to clear any trees still standing.

While they placed most of their effort on fighting the Eastern Province fire, other areas of China were also experiencing abnormal events.

In the Western Provinces, they experienced swarms of locusts, destroying crops and leaving fields bare. The locusts swarmed in as a dark dense cloud ten miles long and on a five miles wide front. They consumed everything in their path, leaving little for harvesting.

The locusts not only attacked the crops but the working animals and workers in the fields, causing many to collapse and eventually die from the endless attacks. The animals would try to run to safety, but eventually collapsed and died as the locusts consumed their remains.

Villagers told Beijing about the locust swarm when they couldn't stop it and saw the damage to crops and land.

Beijing ordered the air force in to spray the locusts. They deployed all spray planes they could get their hands on to slow the swarm of locusts down and kill them, but they had little effect. The swarm would multiply and become more dense and wider, causing several planes that were employed to spray them, to crash as they flew through the dense clouds, jamming the propellers or causing the engines to stop.

The government used napalm bombs to get rid of locust swarms that were preventing workers from harvesting. This not only incinerated the locusts, but owing to the inaccuracies of the piolets, caused farm equipment and buildings to be destroyed.

In the Northern Province, the crops were affected by bad weather in that an abnormal cold snap was encountered. These had the effect of preventing the crops from ripening and the harvesting of the produce. Eventually, the produce will have to be churned back into the soil, as the fruit was not consumable.

The government briefly advised the nation of the cold snap, and that production would be lower owing to these conditions. It did not mention the abnormal cold or that it occurred in summer and that it was a bad omen. The cold also brought on illnesses and a flu like virus struck down many of the population in the province, killing many of the older adults.

Many sought medical help for raspatory illnesses, and a large percentage of the population died of this mysterious illness which spread throughout the region like the plague.

The culmination of these catastrophes was instead of achieving an abundance of crops, China would have to buy from overseas countries to feed its population. It began acquiring from third world countries. However, their produce was of poor quality and many in China asked why they have been forced to accept this lower quality produce.

Television declared that Australia refused to sell its produce to China, or that Australia had a poor year and did not have any crops to sell to China. However, travellers returning from trips to Australia soon made it clear that the government was not telling the truth. The population had to accept the poor-quality produce and understood the Communist were not willing to trade with Australia.

Eventually, Canada, Australia and America were approached to see if they would sell to China. Considering China's previous treatment of these countries and the breach of established Agricultural Agreements, these countries were not willing to accept China's word that they would honour any new agreements made. They had proven to be liars in the past and no one would again accept their word that they would fulfill their contractual obligations.

They forced China to buy through the back door in that a third world country would lodge an order and China would buy the grain from that country. This was double handling and a costly way of trading commodities, but this was the corner China had backed itself into.

The Chinese Government tried several false campaigns to sell the idea that the Government did not cause the shortage of good produce, but the shortage was caused by the refusal of those countries to sell to China. They did not declare why or the history as to why these countries refused to assist China, nor would they reveal China had refused to abide by the free trade agreements that it signed up for. The world viewed China to be an unethical country which would not honour its word.

China moved a motion in the United Nations, declaring Australia, Canada and the United States were countries refusing to sell grain to their starving population and that the UN should force them to sell to China on humanitarian grounds.

The matter was debated extensively in the UN Assembly with the eventual agreement reached that the UN would oversee the shipments and guarantee payment.

They sent grain to China, but the suppliers knew China wouldn't keep the agreement.

CHAPTER 17

Reports that were sent to the Central Bureau advised that the fire had destroyed approximately forty percent of the crops and burned out many villages, destroying farm equipment, sheds and storage of fertilisers used for growing crops. It also had destroyed the irrigation systems in the areas affected, including housing and community centres and hospitals. Approximately fifty thousand people had lost their lives in fighting the fire and not being able to get out of its path. Many were elderly living in villages and hospitals.

Amongst the reports received was one which noted that the fire front had bypassed a village in the Eastern Province, which had a church in the centre of the village. When the fire had surrounded the village and it was of no use to continue fighting in the fields, the residents stopped fighting the fire and gathered around the church to pray.

The report advised that the fire did not touch any of the fields controlled by the villagers and it left them safe with all their crops, buildings, farm equipment and animals in tack.

The National People's Congress, in receiving the report, wanted to know how it was possible for the catastrophe to have bypassed the village. They dispatched a delegation to investigate and report back within a week.

Other reports tabled showed a dismal picture of the Eastern and Western provinces' production and the effect this catastrophe will have on the nation's economy. They agreed that the government will have to spend vast sums of money to rebuild the villages and hospitals destroyed and that a fresh approach would have to be taken. The rebuilding should accommodate a modern China rather than rebuilding what was old and lost. It will have to be in line with an overall plane that will have to be agreed to by the National People's Congress, and reflect a modern China, capable of accommodating industry and commerce and not just agriculture.

A delegation was agreed to, and they wasted no time in making plans to visit the Eastern Province village.

The President did not want to be included in the delegation, as he still believed that the Monk had been incinerated in the fire that burned down the police station. He had firsthand experienced of the explosion and its ferocity and believed no one could have survived the inferno.

Three days later, two helicopters flew into the town centre. One with the delegation, the other with ten armed guards. They demanded the Village People's Committee assemble before them, which was arranged expeditiously, as the guards were not known for their patience.

The Committee sat at the central table and the villagers stood around the outer perimeter listening to what was being said.

The delegate leader said, 'We have come here to find out why your village was spared the ravaging fire that engulfed the surrounding area. What did you do to force the fire to go around you?'

Committee Leader said, 'We did nothing except, seeing that we could not extinguish the fire and that it was gaining intensity, fell on our knees and prayed, and the Lord heard our prays and helped us, making sure the fire did not come close to our village or church.'

The delegate leader said, 'Do you take me for a fool? You must have done something more. What was it you did?'

Committee Leader said, 'We have told you we prayed to God, and he delivered us.'

Delegate Leader said, 'Stop being a fool. Do you expect me to tell the National People Congress that you prayed, and your God stopped the fire? Soon you will tell me He can walk on water. I cannot go back and report what you have told me. You and your villagers will be in trouble if I tell the Congress what you have said. No one will believe you and they will put you in jail for refusing to tell us the truth and for praying. You know it is against the law to pray to anyone other than the President. I again ask you, what did you do to stop the fire from burning down your fields and village?'

Committee Leader says. 'We have told you the truth. Ask anyone in the village and they will tell you the same thing.'

The monk then enters the hall, and they asked him what the villagers did to stop the fire. He repeated what they had already stated to them, but they would not believe him.

After a further frustrating hour of questioning the delegation agreed that they could not get the Committee to reveal the truth so they would take them back to Beijing and arrange for the military to question the men and allow the delegates at the National People's Congress to hear for themselves, the replies given by the Village Committee.

They took the five committee men on board of the helicopter along with the monk and they flew off to Beijing.

Those arrested protested, but the delegates were not willing to go back with the replies given, as they would be considered fools and incompetent in accepting those answers.

The men were worried, as it seems the truth was unacceptable by the delegation and would not be accepted by the National People's Congress, which would place them in danger of being tried and sentenced to death.

When they arrived in Beijing, the men were taken into custody and placed in a cell overnight. The next day, they were brought before the National People's Congress around midday after it was reported that they were not willing to co-operate with the delegation. The chief delegate who attended the village gave a summary to the National People's Congress and then turned to the men and again asked them to explain how they were able to prevent the fire from consuming their fields and village.

The six men looked at each other, not willing to be the first to speak.

The President was taken by surprise and momentarily couldn't find the words as he thought he was looking at a ghost. The President turned to the Monk and said, 'How did you escape from the fire that burned down the police station some months ago?'

'Did you apply the same black magic to avoid the fire that has burned many of the fields in other villages in Eastern Province and in other provinces? How did you come back to life? Were you reborn as the bible declares?'

The Monk was speechless, not understanding the questions the President was asking. He tried to say something but fumbled not knowing how to answer, as he couldn't understand the questions. He did not understand what the President was saying about his death, as he was very much alive. As for the black magic, what black magic was the President referring to?

The Monk explained the situation as best he could and what had happened on that day of the fire and concluded as the committee had stated previously, that when all seemed lost and they could not beat the fire or get on top of it, they all downed tools and went to the church and prayed to God for help.

God heard their prays and directed the fire to go around their village. Not one of their fields was burnt, nor any of their animals or houses destroyed.

There was silence as the Monk spoke and when he stopped, he sat down with all the members of the Congress and the President, staring at them in disbelief.

The President stood up and said, 'How did you manage to be burnt alive and still stand here before the National People's Committee? When did you get resurrected?'

The Monk replied, 'I do not understand your question. I have not died, so I did not have to be resurrected.'

The President said, 'I saw the police station burn down with nothing standing. You and all of those committee members died in the fire. How are you now able to stand before us?'

All in the great hall waited for an answer, but none was given.

No one in the National People's Congress would have accepted whatever the villagers said. The president rose to his feet and made it clear to them that unless they told the truth; they would be thrown into prison along with their families and they would most probably be shot for following religious practices, which are against the law and for practicing black magic to prevent being burnt alive in the fire.'

The President said, 'You see before you men who believe in a God who has scrambled their brains. Their belief is that great that they cannot see how absurd their replies are to our questions. They rely on this invisible God to protect the village and the souls of the villagers. We cannot allow this matter to continue because if we did, other villagers would use the God's excuse in their defence. We can only say that there was a change in wind that on this occasion it turned the fire onto itself, causing it to burn out after burning the area surrounding the village.'

The Monk again repeated that God protected them during the holocaust, and it was their faith that saved them.

As soon as they stated this, the assembly erupted into a mad screaming crowd, demanding they be executed for refusing to tell the truth or provide an appropriate answer.

The president demanded that the guards take them away while others screamed, 'We should shoot them for treason.'

The president stood up and said, 'We cannot allow this village to lie to the National People's Congress and get away with it. They should be made an example of as to what will happen to those who put themselves above The National People's Congress. We should order the destruction of the village and its church, which I understood had already been done, but it appears what were told to us were lies.'

'In fact, we should move to stop all religion in our country and not just Christianity, as it only leads to false reliance on a non-existing God. I am a sufficient God for China and what I do can be seen and questioned by all. We do not have to accept the Bible or its ancient teachings and should outlaw this practice in our country. We should expel all ministers from our country. We do not need missionaries to provide us with false teachings. None of us here believe in a God. We all know there isn't one.'

'If they want to worship someone, they can worship me. I move a motion that the village be destroyed along with its church and to outlaw all religions in China. All missionaries are to cease their work immediately and remove themselves from our country. They have seventy-two hours to get out of our country or they will be arrested and thrown into prison for life. There is to be no more preaching of the Bible, and all monks and ministers are to remove themselves from our country. All those who agree raise your hands.'

There was no one who objected. All raised their hands and voted in favour of the motion.

As the six were being led away, a rumble began under foot, which increased in intensity and the president yelled out, 'Earthquake! Get out of the building.'

Immediately all delegates ran for the doorway but with a full Congress it was not possible for all to get out quickly. Some were trampled underfoot, trying to get out while others fought with those in front of them, preventing them from making their way out.

As for the Monk and five committee delegates, no one cared about them, and they stayed put looking at the great scramble to get out of the building. Everyone was for themselves, and no one cared about any other person. It was a mad scramble to the exit, as everyone expected the building to collapse.

The men sat there for about an hour until all had moved out of the building. More rumbles were felt, so the men decided it was too risky to remain there, so they got up and walked out of the building and made their way out onto the street to see what was happening.

There was damage to the facade of buildings, and some walls had collapsed. Damage had been done to the courtyard and foot paths and there were quite several fallen trees. A building had partially collapsed, but no one was killed.

No one was worrying about the men trampled underfoot. All got away from the area. None were attending to those who were injured. The six stopped to give aid to those injured, but they refused their help, fearing someone will see them and they will be deemed part of the conspiracy.

The men stood there for a while, not knowing what to do. They decided to make their way back to their village and not to stay around to be arrested again. They walked up the street and noted that there were several vehicles which were left abandon as the occupants feared the earthquake.

The Monk got in one of the army vehicles thinking as it was government property; it belonged to the people and therefore no one could accuse him of stealing. The others, seeing what he was doing, got in the back of the truck. He started the engine and drove off in an easterly direction towards their village. He noted the truck had a full tank of diesel, which would enable them to drive home without the need to stop or refuel.

The six at the time did not realise that the truck contained provisions and medical supplies in the back, which would be useful to their province.

The journey was a long one, and it was obvious that an earthquake was responsible for extensive damage.

On their journey, the matter of their escape was raised several times.

The men could not believe that they could walk out of the National People's Congress and make their own way back home without being arrested or challenged. It was obvious the earthquake was an act of God, and He was protecting them and using them in His plan.

The men knew the President wanted to take the glory of China's prosperity for himself, but this was not part of God's plan.

He wanted to run China as if he was God, which God would not allow.

The men thank God for his mercy and protection and asked for his help to get out of this mess, as they knew this would not be the end.

Twelve hours later, the men arrived at the village at the amazement of the locals, who thought they would never see them again for speaking out the truth.

They were greeted with cheers and adulation and eventually all moved to the church to hear what had happened in Beijing and to thank the Lord for their safe return.

The villagers were advised of what the President did in making himself God and that he had ordered the destruction of the village and church, which should take place in the next few days.

They were asked to be observant and if they heard war planes approaching, they were to evacuate themselves and their family to the nearby underground tornado shelters. All were to ensure the shelters had an adequate supply of water and basic provisions, as they might have to stay there for a few days.

The National People's Congress Building was badly destroyed by the earthquake, making it inhabitable. This was to the President's benefit as now he could have an excuse as to why he decided without first seeking opinion from the Assembly.

The President was annoyed that his generals had lied to him about the destruction of the church. He decided once and for all to destroy the village and the church, as previously he assumed this had been done when war planes were ordered in to bomb the church.

He would take personal responsibility and ensure the job was done. For the present he had more important things to attend to regards the earthquake.

Over the next week, the President was flown over the major affected areas of the country and appoint an administrator for each area who was to formulate a plan as to what was needed to fix and recover from the damage.

Administrators in the affected provinces formalised their plans as to what was required to rectify the problems and forwarded these onto Beijing for approval. The plans were compared to each other, and the best approach adopted which was to apply to all affected provinces.

Once the decision was made, this was conveyed to the Peoples Committee in the Provinces, and they were responsible to see that the work was carried out. All bridges and roads were to be repaired or replaced if the damage was extreme. As for the houses occupied by the villagers, these were the responsibility of the occupant and not the Government. They had to be repaired as best as the occupant could afford and do.

Most of the villages had no money and therefore there was a lot of graft where the government allocated funds to repair infrastructure. The cost of the repairs was loaded to ensure the villagers could use some of the money to repair their homes.

CHAPTER 18

S ue sat in her study at home, staring at the wall. She stayed there
for an hour until she was brought back to reality by one of her
children shaking her and screaming out 'Mom'.

It was Saturday, and this was shopping day when the whole family
went to the supermarket and purchased groceries for the week and
any incidentals the kids may need for school.

They attended to the shopping and packed the groceries a way in
the car's boot, then moved on to buying each of the children a new
pair of shoes for school. Once this was completed, it was back home
and housework.

The kids went out to play in the backyard and Sue finished the
vacuuming and washing and then, in the afternoon, a bit of gardening.

The kids came in and had their dinner and bath and went to
watch television while Sue did some work on a brief she was working
on for action against China and their failures to uphold human rights
in that country.

She drafted an affidavit and then stopped to think about where
her life was heading and what was she achieving. She thought about
this for a while and wondered what she was doing with her life. What
was the purpose of her existence? To raise her kids? Surely there must
be more than just that. She thought about it and felt herself again

looking down a deep black hole, into emptiness which she did not want to go back to.

There must be a purpose which no doubt she will find out in the years to come. Surely there must be more to life than just being born and, after a few years, die and achieve nothing. There must be a reason for the struggles and hurt that is suffered. She kept thinking about life and the purpose of her being on the earth and each time she kept coming back to God as a centre point. He created us surely for more than to suffer. Yet, suffering must be a key aspect of life. She realised that in her lifetime she had experienced things that could not be bought such as love, anger, rejection, hurt, embarrassment, and such like. These things cannot be gained, acquired, or taught. They must be experienced. Lived through. So, must bereavement, which is the most hurtful of all experiences and which she recalls made her believe God did not want to know her and had rejected her.

Sue thought about it further and realised what she experienced when James died, and when her parents were killed in mainland China, was what God must have gone through when mankind hung his only son, Jesus Christ, on the cross.

She thought about it more and realised that God had not left her but allowed her to experience feelings which could only be understood by living through them. They could not be bought or taught. She realised that what she went through had a purpose which, over time, would be revealed to her.

Sue clasped her hands together and prayed to God for forgiveness and help to understand his plan and why it was necessary for her to go through the trauma she had. After a minute of pray, she got up and went to put the kids to bed, after which she was determined to attend to the drafting of the affidavit to the Human Rights Commission.

Sue read a story to the kids, and then switched the light off and went to her study.

She again stared into a bottomless black hole. She knew she had to discipline herself to stop slipping back into depression and to concentrate on her work and draft the initial affidavit. It was required by Monday, as it was going to be the prime document used to advance the case and put forward the evidence.

She spent the entire night working on the affidavit. She finished a good first draft and included pages for the evidence. Each sheet contained a brief description of the evidence intended to be presented to support the case.

Sue turned around and saw her husband James siting in one chair in her study, smiling at her as if he was saying well done. She could not believe her eyes and rubbed them. Again, looking at the chair James was sitting in. However, there was nothing there, just emptiness. She realised her mind was playing a trick on her as she was lonely and remembered the conversations she used to have with James, discussing her work and the challenges he faced as a surgeon. She knew James would always be with her.

CHAPTER 19

S ue sat in John's office as he attended to an administrative matter that had cropped up and that needed prompt attention. After giving instructions to his secretary, John came back into his office and sat at his desk, noting Sue was staring out the window, not realising he had come in.

John said, 'Sue, you look as if you have something on your mind. Is something troubling you?'

Sue says, 'Yes, I realise that I have been foolish in blaming God for my misfortunes and have prayed for forgiveness. You said the last time we met that one aspect causing depression was my lack of faith in God, so I have come to see if you would help me, as my depression is getting worse and is affecting my work and home life. I stare into a black hole for long periods and achieving very little.'

John says, 'Mental illness is a biological problem exacerbated by stress in one's life. I assume the stress in your case is the loss of your husband and parents and, as you have previously stated to me, you believe because of your action in Hong Kong has led to them being killed by the Chinese military. You accept that in a democratic country, your actions would not affect your parents and outer family. However, you have stated that you and your husband knew what the Chinese government would do to your family if you continually protested in Hong Kong for your democratic rights.'

'Depression is hard to diagnose, and most people get to know that they are depressed when friends or family notice that they are not themselves such as having trouble getting out of bed, and missing activities or appointments, take a non-caring attitude to life or start speaking about suiciding. '

'Those most at risk in getting depression are women, older adults, those with a personal or family history of depression, chronic stressors, those with other concurrent mental and physical health conditions, low socioeconomic status, and those taking medications that may cause depression, like birth control or some anxiety medications.'

'When you experience a loss of someone close to you, it is normal to grieve and feel down and empty for a period, but life should get better and not control your emotions. With depression, it does just that.'

'For some people, depression is cyclical, and they can eventually recover with no specific intervention while others who suffer depression never seek treatment as they do not want to be considered as mentally ill. What they don't realise is the stigma around depression has mostly gone, and most people recognise it to be a mental illness and do not look down upon the person with depression.'

'While there is no sure-fire way to prevent depression, one of the greatest protective factors for depression is social connection and support. Maintaining healthy friendships and relationships might significantly decrease the likelihood or severity of depreciation.'

'Depression is most likely to occur in adults between the ages of 45 and 65 but of late, most clinicians believe even children who suffer a trauma can become depressed.'

'Also, the chance that an individual will receive care for symptoms of depression is often based on their social situation. Some who are relatively isolated or lacks financial means may be at risk for not getting treatment and fall into deeper depression.'

'The more we can de-stigmatise emotions, the more we can help that person or prevent or slow down the progression of negative emotions.'

'While it has proven no specific diet relieves depression, a healthy diet can help you physically and mentally. We may link certain foods to brain health and support for memory, alertness, and mood. Examples include foods that contain omega-3 fatty acids found in nuts and fatty fish like salmon, antioxidants found in blueberries and broccoli and nutrients like choline found in egg yolk. You should always talk to your local doctor before setting on a plan or if you are changing a plan.'

'I believe you have discussed your condition with your doctor, but still find yourself depressed and unable to relieve the symptoms. Since your problem does not seem to be mental or an imbalance of your body chemistry, then there is only one aspect left, and that is the spiritual or religious aspect.'

'Your doctor is looking after the body, but it is you that is suffering. When I say you, I really mean your soul is hurting, which reflects on the outer body being affected. The outer body is being treated to depress the symptoms but, it is the soul that is hurting. Your doctor cannot cure your depression by treating the body when it is the soul that is the actual cause. In these instances, they can only stabilise your situation hopefully to a degree to enable you to get on with your life.'

'To consider the soul, we must first consider your relationship with God. You touched upon this when we first met this morning.'

'Most people with depression have an aching soul which cannot find peace for what they have done and consider their relationship with God is non-existent or irreparably damaged, and therefore do not seek his help and mercy and turn from Him. They forget God is the creator and will never abandon them, no matter what they have done. He died on the cross, so their sins may be forgiven. All that he asks of them is that they come to him and confess their sins and have faith in Him. He will put them back on the path of righteousness. He has paid the price for their sins and only asks them not to sin again. Just speak to Him and confess your sins and as He has often said in the Bible, "Go and sin no more".'

'Remember Sue, the redeemed soul longs for God. This is part of the natural function of your soul. It is hard coded into the soul. It reaches out to its creator and is sought by God.'

'Those that refuse God or want nothing to do with Him lose aspects of their soul. You can say that over time, the soul is sterilised. God stops seeking them out and lets them go their own way.'

'Some say that they have a better life without God and can achieve more for themselves and their family without worrying about the word of God or what has been stated in the Bible. In these cases, all is well for the individual until he dies. The good times cease, and they appear before God for judgement. Here God says, 'I have created you on earth to serve me, but you turned your back on me and served yourself. You never got to know me during your lifetime and specifically avoided me. All was acceptable to you if the means justified the result, that being self-satisfaction. I declare your judgment is you will exist in Hell for eternity. Your sins are not forgiven, and you continually sinned to achieve what you desired, which now amounts to nothing. Since I do not know you, begone with you to hell.'

'The redeemed soul longs for God, and depression normally intensifies the soul's longing for God. Since God is the source of all healing, it is appropriate that the Christian soul sometimes searches for God more in illness than in health. But the soul reaches out and often cannot find God. Depression increases our longing for the one who heals, yet the disease veils our view of Him.'

'Sue, you must remember mental illness can damage the soul but cannot destroy it. Only humanity can do that.'

'The function of the soul is to be witness to the image of God. The sick soul normally is the soul of the person who does not acknowledge the might of God. This could have something to do with despising God or simply not knowing enough about God. It is those who do not give thanks to God who are soul sick and not necessarily those suffering mental illness. They felt that because of their mental illness or sins that God hides his face from them.'

'When we pray under the strain of illness, God receives our prays and through our prays they bring us closer to Him. He receives our prays whether we are ill or healthy and, in every case, He appreciates your calling upon Him and will always help you.'

'What should you do? You should continue to pray to God, and he will draw closer to you, allowing you to gain faith in Him. No matter what happens, you must not turn from God but explain you do not understand His plan or why you have been singled out to be part of His plan. He will put you in the picture in the future if you do not understand what is happening now. But you must always pray to Him for direction and understanding. Do not refuse to do something or decide by yourself. He will not run your life. You are on the earth to live your life, not for Him to do this for you. However, you can pray to Him, and he will help you make the right decision. Have faith in Him in times of trouble, for He will deliver you.'

'I understand you have made the first step towards this, in accepting Him.'

Sue says, 'Yes, I realise he is the only one that can help me. My doctor can try to fix the body and my mind through medication, but cannot fix the problem of an aching soul. Only Jesus can do this. But I still think back to what has happened in my life and cannot understand why it was necessary to go through all that grief.'

John says, 'Sue, we do not know what He has planned, but let us take one possibility as just that, a possibility. Do you really believe someone who has not experienced what you have can draft the papers and direct the case before the world Human Rights Commission? Do you really think they could express what had occurred and the consequence this had on your lives? I doubt it. You must live through a storm before you can express the feeling and what it did to you. Yes, observation can enable you to describe the consequence but cannot equip you to express what you lived through. Patients, discipline, and endurance are required. You must push despair away and keep it from dominating your life.'

Sue says, 'Yes, you're right. I understand a lot more than what I did before. Please pray with me?'

John says, 'I would be glad to.'

They both held hands and John said a pray out loud, asking the Lord to look after Sue and help her with her depression and work before the Human Rights Commission.

CHAPTER 20

The National People's Congress sat debating figures presented to it which showed China was losing money and would find itself in financial difficulty within three months. No one stood up to criticise the inner circle as they were the most powerful men in China, and all knew what would happen to them and their families if they did.

President says, 'We have had many confrontations with America, and they have threatened to increase tariffs or refuse to trade with China. They refuse to recognise the legitimacy of our naval base in the south China Seas and often provoke our military to where one day they will overstep the mark and we will fire a missile with devastating results for the world.'

'We have over the years acquired a lot of Government Bonds to help the American economy survive during its bad economic crises. Now they show their disrespect for China, which leads me to propose a plan which would stop or forestall their economy and possibly put America into a recession while helping China meet its balance of payment crises and proceed on its capital expansion program.'

Delegate says, 'What balance of payment crises are you referring to? The latest figures show a surplus. How can this be?'

President says, 'Yes, I understand your concern. I will have the figures revamped to show the balance of payment crises but none the less, we require an urgent injection of funds to meet our plans for rectification of the damage the earthquake has done and for growth. We propose to sell fifty percent of our bonds held in America, which would take currency out of the American economy and their share market.'

Delegate says, 'This could cause a repercussion to other country's economies and their stock exchanges and cause our wealth to slump as many have also invested in both American and European stocks.'

President says, 'We have considered that, but do not believe it will get to that point. It will no doubt affect the American economy and possibly reduce it to a depression. I am sure they will stop their boasting when the economy is in a recession or a depression. Most countries will abandon America and they will never recover from their recession unless we gain a lot of their industry to manufacture components for them and get their factory workers back to employment, assembling our components to make their finished products.'

Delegate says, 'It is too risky and could affect our economy in that they are our largest trading partner. You will cripple their economy and possibly decimate ours. I vote not to accept the plan and send it back for reconsideration.'

President says, 'Those who agree with the delegate stand.'

No one stood up to show their opposition.

President says, 'Since you oppose the majority, it is only fit that you be deprived of your position and be replaced by another delegate from your province. Until that happens, I will appoint an alternative to take your place. I dismiss you from the Congress.'

'The majority has voted to accept the plan. It shall be implemented immediately, and fifty percent of all bonds held are to be called up and sold at a discount to ensure we gain the funds needed for our expansion.'

The meeting concluded its assembly, and all delegates made their way home.

As they came out of the building housing the Congress, lying on the steps was the delegate that objected to the plan, with blood spurting out of his head and body. A sniper had shot him.

No one stopped to check on him or lend help. All walked past him as if he were not there.

The next day, his family was gathered up in a military truck and taken to jail to stand trial for treason and a certain death.

The president decided to visit the village and the church before ordering in planes to destroy what was there. He made planes to travel there with military personnel just in case there was trouble.

CHAPTER 21

The president sat back on his sofa, looking at the large television screen. There was a picture of Hitler speaking in a large auditorium and everyone was glued to their seats. He was saying, 'I will do anything to make the fatherland the envy of the world.'

After about a five-minute segment, all in the auditorium spontaneously jumped to their feet, enthusiastically stretched out their right arm and yelled out 'Sig Hail. Sig Hail,' each one trying to scream louder than the person next to them.

The president thought to himself, that man had it right. He controlled his population, and no country would dare to take him on. He brought prosperity to his country, gave the population employment, and armed the nation to repel any country that dared to challenge his plan.

As the screaming intensified, he too stood up and stretched out his arm and yelled out, 'Sig hail, sig hail.'

There was a knock on his door and a servant yelled out, 'Mr President, are you all right?'

The president realised they had heard him. 'Yes, just clearing my throat. I am all right.'

The president turned the television down and thought about Hitler and what he achieved and decided China was to head down the same path and become as great, if not greater, than Germany was in the thirties and forties.

No country in Europe was willing to take up arms against Germany, nor were they willing to call Hitler out for what he was, a murderer of Jews. Every nation turned a blind eye to what was happening and if they were not affected, they did nothing to call out the activities of Germany or the bad things that the country was doing. It would invade Poland and no country came to Poland's defence.

The president thought this is the same thing that is happening with the military base in the south seas and the handling of human rights issues. Some counties like Australia were making some gestures but in the main other countries were not willing to get involved for fear that China would punish them economically and they would suffer.

As for America, it would not support Australia if push came to shove, as they were too far away and they have clarified that America came first. They would protect their territory and make some noise about Australia but, do nothing.

Australia was still reliant on China for trade and would not go it alone against China either military or economically. China owned the Darwin port and could control what movement of vessels occurred at the gateway to Australia. America had a military presence at the port, but this could be taken care of with ease as it was only a few vessels and these could be destroyed by a torpedo or as the Japanese had done in the second world war, just send in planes and bomb the port and the navy vessels anchored there.

The President thought about it and decided that he would allow the American vessels to escape from the port and head for the open sea and then destroy them there, rather than have them block the port. The more he thought about it, he believed we should preserve the Darwin port, as it would be ideal to be used as a port to bring in troops and military equipment on the pretext of protecting Chinese property held in Australia. China owned large geographic areas, farms and industries in Australia and could send in a military force to protect these. In fact, it held close to five percent of the land mass called Australia.

Australia, on the other hand, was not allowed by Chinese law to buy land in China or have a controlling interest in any industry.

The president sat down and thought what stupid people these Australian are to allow a good percentage of their nation's assets to be sold to a foreign power and yet they do not have reciprocal rights. They have let a lot of their mining, infrastructure, and industries such as dairy to be sold off. All for a short-term gain giving the foreign power the rights of sending in their own workers to run the investment rather than achieving employment for Australians.

The President knew these investments had to be made by China and were to be used as China's eyes and ears in Australia. The Australians relied on the Americans for its source of information regards China, whereas the Chinese relied on its own people to advise them what was happening in Australia.

Some who resettled in Australia reported back to China daily of any activities they saw and kept the Chinese Government informed of what was happening in Australia and America. Not only was information being relayed back to China through the Chinese embassy, but also through the internet through encrypted messages.

The Chinese felt so assured of themselves in Australia that they had spies come into the country on the pretext that they were executives of industries that had been bought discreetly in each state. This caused the dismissal of Australian workers from their jobs for they may observe what was going on and declare this to either the police or ASIO. The Chines could not allow this to happen so each worker was dismissed and replaced by a Chines import. One that held allegiance to China.

The Chines did not just rely on its own people for information only. They would approach naturalised Australians of Chinese descent, particularly the ones who worked in the information technology (IT) divisions of large corporations or researchers in medical science area and threaten them that if they did not co-operate and provide them with information, they would have their relatives back in China arrested and tried on espionage charges which would mean they would be shot or imprisoned for twenty or more years.

Some local Chinese who believed in Australian democracy paid the price and went publicly thinking if they shamed the Chines

Government that they would not follow through with their threats, but they found out this was not the case. Within a few weeks of rejecting the approaches of the Chinese Government they heard about the arrest of their parents or the killing of a relative while trying to escape arrest.

To be fair, the Chines Government would arrest the relatives and make sure this information was sent back to those in Australia. They had a second chance to co-operate. If they did, their relatives would be released, but if they did not, then they would never hear from them again and would suffer the mental anxiety and guilt feeling for the rest of their lives.

Some went to the Australian Government with the information which at first was looked at with amazement, as if this cannot be true. No Government would do this to its own people.

The Australian government was naïve in thinking this way and after several its citizens reported what was happening to their relatives or that they were missing, they realised there may be some truth in what was being said.

The Chines government also had military trained men and woman at their embassies to protect their key personnel, and to ensure those who were a threat to China were discreetly eliminated. In short, they were assassins under the pretext of being diplomatic personnel or there to protect their embassy. They were there to eliminate any opposition to what Chine planed.

The Australian Government would once a year revoke an embassy employee's right to remain in the country, but this was not a genuine effort to protect homeland boarders but to look good, for the person they would nominate to send back to China would be someone that the Chines Government wanted back in China for health or family reasons and not that the person was caught spying or was a threat to Australian. It was a publicity stunt by the Australian Government which, while they thought was a good ploy, did not pass the pub test and most Australian knew what was happening.

The President knew Europe would not support Australia as China had invested heavily into their economy and that they would be inclined to look at the "Rubbles" rather than 'What was a right thing to do.' They had failed the world with Hitler, and they would again fail the world when it can to China's push for world dominance.

The President knew Germany had no choice but to dominate the world by military means only, whereas China had already dominated the world economically and this alone would lead to its success.

Unlike the Germans, the Chinese dominance of world trade would allow it to control countries through their economies. Military would follow, to control unrest, but not to invade. The Chines knew they could operate under the laws of a country and if these conflicted, then they could have the laws changed to allow them to achieve their goals. If you have the money, you can always buy what you want. The Chinese have found that principles go out the window, when enough money is offered.

CHAPTER 22

The President got into one helicopter and signalled for all the units to be airborne. Within minutes, five helicopters took off for the Eastern Province to check out the village and church before they ordered in bombers to destroy what was there.

The flight took two hours, and it covered much of the fertile land, showing the devastation that had occurred. It was obvious when they approached the village that the area was fertile and green and not affected, as were the other areas.

The President stepped out of his helicopter after the army assembled and lined up to protect him should anyone start trouble.

The villagers all came out to greet the President and were very vocal in cheering him on and welcoming him to their village. Once the speeches were made, the President sat down in the community building to discuss with the Village Committee and Monk what had been decided.

He explained the National People's Congress had decided to destroy the village and church as a sign of what will happen to any province that refused to co-operate, as was the case here.

The Monk looked stern and stared at the President. He stood up and addressed the President, hesitating for a few seconds.

The Monk said, 'You say that all religions are to be eliminated from our country and you are to be made a God of the people. I had a dream last night which involves you and the decision you have made.'

'First, I was told to advise you that you will not destroy our village. Our God the creator will not allow you to do this.'

'Second, I am to ensure you know what happened to a great king some years ago called Necabukanisa.'

'He ruled Persia, a great powerful country, and no country would stand up against him. Yet God taught him a lesson by making him live with the animals for seven years before he pleaded to be reinstated to his previous glorious position. Eventually, after seven years with the animals, he was allowed to resume his position as king of Persia.'

'From that point on, he worshipped our God and made sure that everyone he came across understood the power of our God. You also will be taught this lesson if you try to destroy our village and church. This is the message I have been given to convey to you.'

The President waited, looking worried. He said, 'Your imaginary God does not scare me, nor does he exist. He is only in your head. You are mad and you will see your village destroyed because of your stupidity.'

With that, the President stood up and ordered everyone to prepare to be airborne. He intended to return to Beijing immediately. He had heard enough to conclude he could not persuade the villagers to accept there was no God and to declare the truth. He tried to bribe them, and they still would not turn against their God.

The President returned to Beijing and immediately convened a meeting of the National People's Congress to take place mid-week.

The National People's Congress assembled for an urgent meeting, and all were in attendance for fear someone may accuse them of something, which would lead to their demise.

The President rose to address the meeting and said, 'I attended the Eastern Province village, and they refuse to answer our questions regards their farming practices and refuse to acknowledge that there is no God except the People's Congress. I therefore move that the village be bombed into oblivion as punishment for their refusal to tell us the truth about their farming practices and their refusal to reject their God. Is there anyone who would object to this motion?'

There was silence for a moment, then one delegate stood up and said, 'I know of the village and of the Monk there. What does he say?'

The President said, 'It is irrelevant what he says as all know this man to be insane. He advises that their increase in productivity comes from their prays to their God and their God has made it clear that he will not allow the village nor the church to be bombed, as we intend to do. We must show strength here, as others will try to use this tactic against us. There is no God except the People's Congress.'

The delegate stood up and said, 'I understand the Monk has said more to you, which it seems you are refusing to divulge. I understand that should we vote on the destruction of the village and church that all delegates will be struck down with an invasive virus which will produce a violent rash over all our bodies, and this rash will develop into an itch which will be extremely painful, and which will drive the person mad.'

The President said, 'I take nothing the Monk says as true and believe this is merely to scare us. It is only witchcraft.'

Delegate says, 'Witchcraft you say, then vote to destroy the village and pay the price.'

The President says, 'Enough of this fear mongering. All those in favour of bombing the village and church raise your hand.'

Momentarily, there was only one hand raised that being the Presidents. Then there appeared another and then another until there were approximately ninety percent of the Committee in favour of destroying the village.

Those against the proposal looked at each other, fearing reprisal if they did not raise their hands. They sat there in full view of the other delegates. Not knowing what to do. Accept what the Monk has said or ignore this and risk the curse.

The President stood up and said, 'You have shown yourselves to be followers of this false God and against the People's Congress. You will no longer hold your position in this Congress, and you are to step down and we will appoint delegates to take your place.'

The delegates knew that upon leaving the building they and their families would be arrested and could be shot or jailed on made up charges. However, it was too late to change their minds as the vote had been taken.

The President stood up and said, 'We order the air force to bomb the village and destroy the church as a matter of urgency and the minister is to take personal charge to ensure they fulfil these orders within forty-eight hours.'

As the President spoke, it became noticeable that a rash was appearing on his face, hands and down his neck. Other committee members who voted for the proposal also developed the same rash on their body and each looked around and could see that those who voted for the proposal were being affected while those who voted against the proposal were not.

A committee member immediately stood up and said, 'Mr President, I withdraw my vote for the destruction of the village and church.' This was followed by other members doing the same thing until all members had withdrawn their support. The only one left not withdrawing his support was the President who noticeably became sicker by the minute until someone called for an ambulance.

The President refused to back down and declared that the village was still to be bombed off the face of the earth. As he uttered those words, he collapsed, and no one wanted to touch him, so they left him where he fell.

The ambulance arrived and immediately the paramedics put on protective gear before touching the President. They turned him on his back and could see the rash had covered all of his body. They put him on a stretcher and lifted him up to be carried out of the building. They took him to the ambulance and loaded him up into it for transporting to the hospital.

At the hospital they examined the President but could not recognise the rash nor what had caused it. They gave the President steroids to reverse the rash, but nothing would work.

At the National People's Congress the deputy president took control and immediately stood up and said, 'we had voted, but then it seems the committee has withdrawn its vote and therefore the bombing is not to take place. Well, I have decided to follow through with the previous vote and will order the bombing of the village and destruction of the church.'

As soon as he spoke the words, he was struck down with the rash which covered all of his body. The ambulance was again called for, but this time took longer to arrive as they had been further away.

The paramedics immediately put on protective equipment and took out a stretcher from the ambulance and walked into the main hall. They turned up to where the deputy was lying and turned him over. He was not breathing, and they noticed his rash. They felt for a pulse but could not find any and pronounced him dead. They loaded him onto the stretcher and removed him from the building. They drove to the morgue and put him in a body bag and into cold storage for autopsy examination.

The next member in line stood up as soon as the paramedics took the speaker's body away and said, 'I believe it appropriate not to decide this matter today and suspend any further decision until we have considered our options. All agree, raise your hands.'

All attendees raised their hands, and the vote was declared unanimous.

CHAPTER 23

The President lay in hospital with a server rash which had developed into boils, and no one knew how to treat it. All known medications and treatments were tried and found to be ineffective. The President lays in a numb state with a high dose of painkillers to ease the pain. The current deputy president calls a meeting of the National People's Congress to gain a census as to what is to be done with the matter of religion and the church. Delegates refused to attend the meeting without the Monk and local Committee members of the Eastern Province being present.

The deputy president goes to the village himself to speak to the locals and the Monk.

Three helicopters with armed troops land in the town square and the deputy President disembarked from his helicopter and walked to the general hall where he was greeted by the head of the local people's committee. The Monk was not present as he was in church holding a pray meeting.

Deputy President said, 'I have come here to see your prosperity for myself and decide what is to be done to the village and its occupants. Our National People's Committee has yet to decide on this matter.'

The local head of the village said, 'We understood they have decided to leave this matter as it is, with no further action to be taken.'

Deputy President said, 'No we still have to get down to why you can harvest a record volume of crops and see if we can use the process nationwide.'

The head of the local people's committee said, ' We have already explained the reason, but you and your people refuse to accept our explanation.'

Deputy President said, 'No we do not refuse to accept your explanation but find it hard to accept what you are saying as we cannot meet this God nor talk to Him. No one accepts your explanation and believe you are using black magic on the National People's Congress, to prevent the village from being destroyed.'

At that time, the Monk walked in and, on hearing the Deputy President, said, 'The Lord has decided to teach you and your unfaithful lot a lesson as to who has the greater power, your National People's Congress, or God. From midnight tonight rain will fall constantly over the land except on our village. We will get our normal amount of rain, but we will not experience the volumes that the rest of the country will experience. The rain will fall constantly until your National People's Congress meets to declare our Lord is more powerful and is God over all the lands.'

Deputy President says, 'That will never happen. Our National People's Congress is Lord over the Land and decides what is to happen.'

The Monk says, 'You have much to learn, and it seems you will not accept the word of our God, so He will not spare you nor respond to your pleas. You will have to seek him out before he will listen to you. But you have forgotten the curse he had placed on your National People's Congress and on your President who still lays in hospital as a sign of what you could have become if you do not change your ways.'

Deputy President says, 'We have sought advice from our schools of science who say that the rash is merely some bacteria which has spread to all members of Congress. It went just as quick as it came. We have it under control and the only one that still has the rash is the President, who seems not to make progress but still lays in agony. They have asked me to bring you to him so you can remove his curse.'

Monk says, 'You think this is some black magic rather than the work of the Lord? I will not go with you as I believe you will not return me home but again throw me in prison.'

Deputy President says, 'you have my word that we will return you home uninjured and promptly. We only want you to remove the curse from our president.'

Monk says, 'I cannot remove the curse, only God can do this.'

Deputy President says, 'Then you better speak to Him and get it removed, otherwise your village will experience destruction and they will kill all in the village.'

The Monk says, 'As I have stated, only God can remove the curse. No one other than God can do it.'

Deputy President says, ' They have instructed me to bring you to him, so that is what I am going to do. Guards, take him to the helicopter.'

With that, the troops arrested the Monk and bound his hands and led him to the helicopter and it flew off back to Beijing.

Once they arrived at Beijing, they disembarked from the helicopters, and the Deputy President and the Monk were driven to the hospital.

The Monk entered the room and noticed that the President was motionless and was in great pain. He stood there for a minute looking at the swollen body, not knowing what he could do as the most important medical minds had been brought together to consider the President's situation and what they could do to ease his condition and pain. After standing there for a few minutes, the Monk bowed his head and said a pray over the President. As soon as he finished, he stepped back and noticed the rash was subsiding and began slowly to clear up from the face and neck of the President. A nurse came in and she noticed the rash was subsiding and clearing from the President's body. She immediately went out and got a doctor who came in and stood there for a few minutes, noticing the rash clearing up from the face and body of the President.

Within ten minutes, the President opened his eyes and spoke to the doctor congratulating him on finding a cure. The doctor ordered the Monk out of the room and began taking more blood samples for analysis and looking at the monitor, which showed the President was improving. Within an hour, the rash had gone from the President's body, and he no longer needed pain tablets or oxygen. The doctors were not willing to tell the President the truth that they did nothing to assist his condition other than pump him with painkillers to keep him sedated.

The Monk found himself in Beijing, with no accommodation or money or means of getting back home. He walked the streets, trying to think how he was going to get out of this mess. As he walked along the street, he noticed the large number of military vehicles with keys in the ignition. He remembered the last time they brought him to the Assembly when the earthquake occurred, and he took a vehicle with members of his village and drive home. He decided that since there was no other means available to him, he would once again take a vehicle and drive home as he did previously.

He walked up the street until he saw a vehicle which had a red cross over it. He looked inside and noticed medical supplies and took this one, as the village could benefit from the supplies, especially the very young and elderly. He got in and started the engine and drove off to the Eastern Province.

After driving through the evening and night, he pulled over and to take a nap as he was falling asleep and was scared he would have an accident. He moved to the back of the truck and shifted some supplies to one side and laid on some tarpaulins that were placed over the supplies and fell asleep. He was interrupted by the sound of what seemed to be water dripping off the truck. He looked out and saw that it was pelting down. He looked at his watch and it was five past twelve. Just as the Lord said it would.

He got up, moved to the driver's seat, started the truck and drove off towards the Eastern Province.

One hour from home, he noticed the rain had stopped, and the road was dry and firm, allowing him to pick up speed.

Two hours later, he drove into the village, to the amazement of all the villagers.

The president made a full recovery and took leadership of the Country. No one advised him of the monk or what had really transpired.

CHAPTER 24

Sue looked anxious as she waited in the Boardroom for Jerry and the team to assemble to discuss her affidavit.

After about ten minutes, Jerry and several other solicitors walked into the Boardroom. Jerry moved to the head of the table and stated, 'Thank you for attending. You all have reviewed Sue's affidavits. There is the main affidavit containing the facts and the affidavits of the witnesses to the events who will attend the hearing and give evidence. We also have a documentary showing video of what happened which has been put together by a well-known and respected director who will swear that he has used footage of scene from film crews who were on the scene at the time of the demonstrations. Has anyone got any comments to make?'

One lawyer stood up and asked questions regards some accusations raised particularly as to the credibility of those witnesses who have agreed to give evidence as to what occurred.

Sue said, 'They have lost loved ones and believe it is their duty to tell what had happened to them and the treatment they received at the hands of the Chinese authorities.'

Other members of the team raised their opinion, some were in support of the document while others raised issues against it. The primary concern was what the Human Rights Committee was going to do once they found China was in breach of the international charter on human rights. They would not punish China other than shame them for its treatment of citizens of Hong Kong, refusing them the right to free expression. They could find China acted irresponsibly and criminally in shooting those who demonstrated or imprisoned those who were arrested for demonstrating.

After several hours, a list of amendments was compiled, and Sue was to amend her affidavits to include these. They agreed that once the document was amended, it would be signed by Jerry and filed with the International Human Rights Commission along with the affidavits of the witnesses and the affidavit of the film director as to the authenticity of the film footage.

The affidavits were very critical of China and raised alarming questions about how China handled the protests and demonstrations in Hong Kong and compared this to what had happened at Tiananmen Square protests and massacres. The methods employed to quash resistance there were the same as used in Hong Kong, which was intending to kill off any protests. Evidence was submitted that live ammunition was used to control the demonstrators in Hong Kong, with many being killed or arrested. China did not care about the rights of any individual. It only cared about its purpose, that being to crush the demonstrations and bring the demonstrators to their knees. They did not care that they killed indiscriminately, some without justification. It wanted a result quickly and didn't care about how it was achieved.

The affidavit also touched upon the persecution of the Uyghur Muslims and the intent to either transform them into a non-religious sect or eliminate them altogether.

The International Human Rights Commission charter is to give to all people the right to free speech, religion, association. Rights inherent to all human beings, regardless of race, sex, nationality, language, religion, or any other status. Human rights include the right to life and liberty, freedom from slavery and torture, freedom of opinion and expression, the right to work and to education. According to the International Human Rights Commission, everyone is entitled to these rights, without discrimination.

China does not abide by the charter of the International Human Rights Commission and does what its committee decides, irrespective of the consequences befalling its population. However, nations that abide by the International Human Rights Commission invariably place sanctions on countries that do not conform to the Commission's charter.

Sue went back to her desk and, during the day, amended her main affidavit to take into account the amendments requested by the other members. She attached a list of cases that had been referred to and attached a separate list, noting the legislation that the Chinese military had breached in carrying out the government's orders.

It was late in the evening when Sue completed her work, so she decided to go home and hand the documents to Jerry the next day. Sue locked up her document and walked to the lift. She went down to the car park in the building's basement and walked to her car. As she approached it, she noticed a man standing near her car. He was of Asian appearance and well dressed, with a coat over his arm. She ignored him, hoping he would walk away, but he didn't. She got to her car and was trying to find her keys in her bag when the man approached her and said, 'You have drafted some kind of document which will embarrass my government. They have asked me to advise you that if you continue to discredit them, we will be forced to take action that will cause some of your friends and colleagues being hurt or worse. This is just a friendly warning.' The man then turned and walked a couple of yards to a car which was driven up to collect him. He got into the car, and it drove off.

Sue was shaking with fear and went back and report it to Jerry. She got in the lift and waiting until she reached his floor. She got out and ran to Jerry's office, collapsing into a chair, shaking with fear.

Jerry asked her what had happened, but she could not speak for some minutes as she sat there trembling. After about ten minutes, she could tell Jerry what had happened, and the threat conveyed to her.

Jerry immediately called the police who, after a half an hour, arrived and began interrogating Sue.

Jerry advised the police what they had been working on and that they had held a final meeting that day to complete their application to the International Human Rights Commission.

Detective said, 'Sue, what did the man actually say to you?'

Sue said, 'well I don't know what he said to me. I was too scarred. I was thinking, is he going to shoot me as I thought he had a gun in his hand that the coat covered? But what he was implying was that some of my colleagues working on this application to the International Human Rights Commission would be targeted or, worse, could be found dead and that I should reconsider my intentions and discontinue any further action.'

Jerry said, 'How did he know we were working on the submission to the International Human Rights Commission?'

Detective said, 'It seems one of your team members is a spy and has advised the Chinese government about what is happening. They most probably conveyed to them what had been agreed to at your meeting and have passed on to them a copy of your affidavit. I will need a list of who was at the meeting so we can check with our federal police to see if they know anything.'

Jerry provided the detectives with a list of who was at the meeting and their position in the firm.

The detectives requested Jerry call a meeting of the group tomorrow morning and allow the detectives to attend so they could ask questions. This was agreed to.

Detectives said, 'We can do no more tonight. We will arrange for the police to increase their patrol around your home, Sue, during the night to make sure no one pays you an unexpected visit. We will accompany you to your car and see you drive off with no further problems.'

With that, Sue made her way out of the office and waited for Jerry, who packed up his papers and both Sue and Jerry, accompanied by the two detectives, made their way to the car park and each drove off to their respective homes.

The next morning Jerry arranged for all the team to again assemble in his office and advised them of what had happened last night to Sue and introduced them to the detectives.

The detectives had already sent a list of attendees to the Federal Police who, with the aid of ASIO, prepared a list of potential persons that could have leaked the information to the Chinese.

Detectives said, 'We believe someone from this group has passed information onto the Chinese Government. Would that person like to advise the group who they are before we start our interrogation of you?'

No one stepped forward, so they agreed the detectives would use one of the unused offices to interrogate those who were present. They spent all day and spoke to everyone who attended the meeting, but no one owned up to being the villain. At the end of the day, the detectives left without knowing who was the culprit.

Meanwhile, Sue had checked her affidavits and film documentaries and took everything up to Jerry's office. Jerry checked the amendments had all been made and signed the affidavit. He put everything in a security satchel and phoned for it to be collected for delivered to their colleagues in the Netherlands who were to lodge the documents with the Commission.

Sue went back to her office to resume her normal days' work.

CHAPTER 25

America was China's largest trading partner, and the economy was booming, causing more goods to be manufactured in China and shipped to America.

The Chinese Government did not want to lose face with its own people in not taking the steps to show the Americans who really were in control of their economy. But it also did not want to cripple its own economy.

To slow the American economy down would reduce demand for Chinese goods and slow the Chinese economy down and slow the transition process from the country to the city where most of the manufacturing was done.

The Chinese Government knew it had too many people on the land farming as they did years ago and following traditional practices. These days with modern practices and machinery, one man can take the place of twenty currently attending to agricultural practices and unless industry was developed, and they were gainfully employed there would be many people unemployed in years to come which politically could cause problems for the Communist party.

It would take clear thinking to get the balance right internally while not crippling its major markets.

The Chinese president decided not to go too heavy in selling the American bonds, but just enough to scare the politicians in America, while not hurting its economy, a rather delegate balance, which the President of China believed he could handle.

They sold the American bonds on the open bond market to bond traders in half a billion dollar lots at a discount to ensure the interest rate was higher than any other secure investment on the market.

The bonds were in demand and bought up by prospective investors throughout the world, since bank interest rates were relatively low compared to the rate that could be gained through the bonds and they were secure. In fact, the Chinese Government underestimated the demand and oversold, resulting in liquidity being withdrawn from the American market.

It did not take long for interest rates to be increased by the Feds and small businesses found themselves not being able to get cheap loans, which were needed to keep their businesses ticking over.

As businesses sold down their stock holdings, they did not have the cash or credit to restock nor were they able to get bank loans, so they went backwards.

It was not long before confidence dropped, and household expenditure was curtailed. Businesses in America were losing money and since demand had dropped off, they dismissed staff, which resulted in an increase in the number of people seeking unemployment benefits in America.

It was not long before China realised it had done the wrong thing in selling more bonds than first intended, as this move would adversely affect the American and Chinese economies.

The American Federal Reserve could see what China was trying to do and that it would force the American economy into depression if they allowed this to happen.

They also noted that the Chinese were the ones selling the bonds and understood that since they could not win politically, they would try to cripple the American economy. It was agreed to hold a meeting with the President of the United States to ensure a co-ordinated plan was developed to send a decisive message back to Beijing.

They held a hasty meeting comprising the President, Vice President, head of defence, Secretary of State and Federal Reserve.

All agreed it was China who was the perpetrator, and it seemed as they overestimated the demand for high term instruments in the low-rate economy of America.

After much debate, it was agreed to protect the American economy while allowing the Chinese to suffer at their own hands. A plan was devised that commercial loans would be issued by the Federal Reserve at low interest rates to corporations that could prove their solvency and long-term viability.

The loans were to be paid back within five years or rolled over at a new rate. Those individuals who were not incorporated but had assets could also access the cheap loans, so long as they could allow the registration of a mortgage or charge over their assets.

Individuals and companies that had bank loans could borrow additional funds to pay off their bank loans and merged their loans into one. Those that could meet none of these criteria could still borrow on production of contracts, proving they needed the money and agreeing on repayments being made on an agreed term basis.

It was further agreed that the banks would become agents for the Government and would receive a commission on every loan made. They would also be penalised at a higher percentage for any loans made that resulted in a loss. It was therefore in their interest to ensure the loans were for viable purposes or projects as they would get one percent commission for every loan earned and administered, but the penalty was five percent if the loan resulted in default, bankruptcy, or liquidation.

They agreed the Federal Reserve would print more money to make these loans and that the loans were only to be made available to companies registered in America and who had their headquarters in the States. Companies who were operating in US with headquarters in Singapore or elsewhere could not gain benefit of these loans nor companies who exported over fifty-one percent of their manufacture to China or likewise imported parts totalling over fifty-one percent of their cost of manufacture excluding labour cost.

It was also agreed to prevent loans to be made to companies who were established in China to manufacture for the US markets or manufacturing components in China for assembly in America.

It established a policy to levy a special tariff of three hundred percent on American companies manufacturing in China and exporting components to America. A special loan would be given to these companies if they wanted to transfer their production back to America and re-establish themselves back home rather than provide employment and profitability to Chinese workers.

It was further agreed to allow companies to write off their research and development costs over a five-year period so they could re-establish new technology once back in America, and to ensure they could manufacture at the same or at a better price than what they were doing while based in China with their cheap labour cost. The technology was not to be sold to the Chinese and had to be developed in America and not in China.

The Chinese never foresaw these measures and were quite surprised to see the Americans react as they did.

The American President went before the United Nations and outlined in a speech what China was doing and the retaliation America had adopted to ensure its economy would not suffer.

The Chinese declared emphatically America had misunderstood China's position and that all that China was trying to achieve was to get US currency to ensure it could meet its obligations.

The European nations knew where the truth lay and had been warned not to go to America's aid as the same misfortune may fall upon them. They knew what China was up to and were glad to see they were caught out and so decisively dealt with.

China was caught with its pans down and within a few months was facing an extreme slowdown of its economy.

The National People's Congress met to get an update on what had transpired from selling its hoard of American Bonds. They had heard the American economy was slowing down and that corporate loans had been harder to get. They were not told what this had done to the Chinese economy and the actual effect this would have long term on the Chinese economy.

The meeting ended with the Chinese President declaring the Chinese economy was on target and that it had exceeded all growth expectations. He did not or was unwilling to tell the delegates what was around the corner and the predicted decline that was expected from the next quarter.

The Americans knew the Chinese Government would never declare it was caught out and they would always project themselves as successful when, in fact, they failed. The Chinese take this position to ensure there was no loss of face.

To ensure everyone knew what was happening; American declared at the United Nations, the steps they had taken to confront what China was doing and what they foresaw were the consequences of such actions, not only to America but world trade.

The Chinese Government declared what America was saying were lies and refused to report the truth back to China. This would allow them to tell untruths at the Congress blaming everyone else except themselves.

Over the next quarter, America's economy stabilised owing to the economic measures introduced preventing China's attempt to force a depression on America.

As more and more American companies closed their production unit in China and came back to the State, the better the American economy became, and it was not long before America again achieved full employment.

As for China's economy, it went from bad to worse, with high unemployment being felt but yet not declared. 'The great economic prosperity,' floundered and went in reverse, forcing the President to declare China was part of the world contraction and its expansionary plans would have to be put on hold until the economy improved.

The delegates at the congress knew what was happening but feared to say anything as their families may suffer. They knew their president was not up to the task when push came to shove. It was alright to confront a poor country and force policy on them, but when you try it on one of your own size, especially one that can push back, then you have a different result.

Companies in Europe saw what America did and did the same, forcing companies back on shore and boosting up their manufacture and reducing their social security bills.

China was the loser, and its people paid for the misjudgement by its leaders. Many found themselves unemployed and being forced to seek help from family members, as the government did not pay for welfare.

CHAPTER 26

The President looked out of his window as the rain pelted down. It had been raining constantly for three weeks non-stop. All the crops that were going to be harvested were rotting in the fields, it being too wet to use heavy machinery to harvest them.

The provinces reported they could not get their machinery out to harvest their crops and if the rain persisted, there will be no crops to harvest as they would all rot in the field. China was looking at a situation where it had now moved from harvesting a record crop to having to import crops to feed its population. This would prove difficult as China had broken its promises made in the free trade agreements with various countries and these countries were not prepared to accept the word of the Chinese government again. If they wanted to buy food from these counties, China had to pay up front and was forced to buy at a premium rate as it could not be trusted.

The only province that reported a record harvest was the Eastern Province, which had not experienced the flooding that was affecting the other provinces.

The President entered the National People's Congress and took his seat. After the formalities, he was asked to report on the economy and what the future quarter was looking like. He rose to his feet and stood looking at the assembly, knowing he had lost the confidence of the members.

President said, 'I have received reports from the provinces, declaring the continual rain has caused flooding and is preventing the crop from being harvested. It is reported that if the rain persists, the crop will decay, and it will have to be ploughed back into the ground. We would then be forced to buy crops from other nations, which would affect our balance of payments and currency reserves.'

A delegate stood up and said, 'Mister President, I understand things are worse than what you have told us. My understanding is that many countries are insisting on their companies closing their manufacturing sites in China and transferring their manufacturing plants back to their home country causing unemployment in China to increase and this coupled with the rain and lost opportunity to harvest a bumper crop has caused China into a terrible economic situation. I also understand that the cause of this started from your attempt to teach the American a lesson by selling bonds to cripple their economy. I also understand that the rain was a direct attempt by you to take the place of God, and to outlaw Christianity and all other religions. You have brought this upon us trying to make a God of yourself.'

The President rises and said, 'Your information is totally wrong and as usual when things go right, everyone wants the glory but when they go bad everyone looks for a scapegoat. Let us put this to a vote. All those who have lost faith in me as president raise your hands.'

The President turns around and could see the delegate that was speaking had raised his hand. There were four other delegates who raised their hands, but upon seeing they were a minority immediately lowered their hand.

President said, 'You are the only one that has this view and is objecting to my administration of the economy. I would suggest the province you represent elects another member to the Congress to replace you. I see that the real problem is with religion and not me or my administration. It is the monk's God that has caused this rain, and the only way to stop it is to destroy the village and church, which we should have done some time ago. We must show who is in charge here. Who really has the power?'

'I order the minister of defence to bomb the village and church into oblivion, and once this is done, I am sure the rain will stop, as no doubt the Monk and the villagers have caused this. As the President spoke, the roof of the building dipped and pieces began to fracture and break off, falling to where the delegates were seated. Then, without warning, the ceiling collapsed, and water flooded into the National People's Congress. Many of the delegates who were seated were crushed or maimed as the roof caved in. The rain increasing in intensity. The hall being flooded. Amongst those injured was the President, who was hit on the head by a flying piece of concrete, knocking him to the ground while another piece of slab fell on top of him, pinning him to the ground.

Delegates rushed out, not caring to help those who were injured. Their only concern was to save themselves. The rain was relentless and intensified, flooding the hall to about one foot from the floor. Soldiers rushed in to see if they could save the President. After searching under slabs of concrete, they located him, and the guards grabbed him by the shoulders and pulled him out, noting he was unconscious. As soon as they got him outside, they called for medical help, but no one came, so they quickly bundled him into an army truck and drove off towards the hospital.

Upon arriving at the hospital, they quickly ordered the staff to bring a stretcher for the President and to rush him into a room where he could be examined by doctors. No rooms were available, so they rushed him into an operating theatre. Two doctors were passing by who were grabbed and pushed into the operating theatre and ordered to examine the President.

The doctors quickly examined him but could not find any injury but to be certain, they ordered a body CT scan. After about two hours, they transferred the President from the operating theatre to a private room. Soon afterwards, the CT scan was handed to the doctors, and they reviewed them. They mutually agreed that no bones had been broken, and all that had happened was a falling piece of concrete knocked the President out. They put him on a drip and gave him oxygen to stabilize his breathing and bandaged his head wound. After an hour, the president showed signs of coming to and the doctors saw that his blood pressure and oxygen level had improved.

The President came around and even though he was still groggy, wanted to know what had happened. A soldier briefed him, and he was told by a doctor to rest. He wanted to speak to his deputy and ordered that he be brought to the hospital. He laid back, as he knew this would take some time.

After about an hour, a soldier came in with an officer and the President was told that his deputy was killed by a falling piece of concrete and that thirty members of the National People's Congress were also killed when the roof collapsed on them.

The President asked who was in charge and was advised no one had taken this role.

The President sat up in bed thinking about what had happened and resumed his role as president. He ordered that his clothes be brought to him so he could get up and resume his role. He intended to pay a visit to the Monk to order him to stop the deluge. He ordered the officer to arrange for helicopters to be available with troops so he could go to the Eastern Province.

The president swung his legs off the bed and tried to stand up, but fell to the floor. The doctors quickly ran to his aid and got him on his feet. He was advised not to get out of bed until he had time to recover. He disagreed but agreed to stay in hospital for the day and to make the trip to the Eastern province tomorrow.

The officer agreed that would be preferable, as it would give them time to get things ready for the flight. He ordered that two soldiers were to stand guard over the President and at no time was anyone allowed to enter without the permission of the President. He then left to make the arrangements for the flight the next day.

CHAPTER 27

The affidavits were lodged with the International Human Rights Commission and as a result, a date was set for the first directional hearing, which was to be in approximately three months' time.

A copy of all the lodged documents were served on the Chinese embassy, who initially refused to accept them. However, with the United Nations intervention, they accepted them and forwarded them onto Beijing.

Beijing informed the Court that it did not recognise the Commission and would not attend.

One month later, Sue receives a telephone call from one witness advising they intend to withdraw their affidavit and would not be attending the hearing on personal grounds.

Sue called the people involved and arranged for a meeting in Jerry's office. They attended and after some hard talk, advised that their relatives back in China had been told that should they take part in the case, their relatives would be arrested and thrown in prison or worst found guilty on a cropped-up charge and sentenced to death.

This applied to two witnesses who withdraw from the hearing. They could accept what would happen to them, but not what would happen to their relatives back in Hong Kong.

A few days later, Sue received a phone call from a relative of another witness, who advised that a Chinese soldier had shot her father while he sat in his car, ready to drive off to work in the morning. The police were investigating the shooting but had no leads other than it seemed to be a professional job by someone who knew what they were doing.

Other witnesses phoned Sue to advise her they had been approached and told that they would be killed if they didn't withdraw their affidavits. Some agreed to do so, while others refused to be intimidated and insisted on being able to have their day in court.

All witnesses were placed on police protection and most changed their address.

Sue advised the Court of what was happening and that the witnesses were being intimidated. She arranged for a Barrister to appear before the Court to seek permission for all affidavits to be recognised by a registration number and the signed copy of the affidavit were locked up under security and each witness given a number which appeared on their affidavits and other documents so the Chinese would not know who the witness was and could not threaten them.

Sue also received threatening phone calls and messages on her phone but refused to be intimidated.

Sue was out shopping with her children, when two men came up to the youngest child and picked her up and tried to run off with her in hand. One shopper in the shopping centre saw what had happened and ran after the men. The one holding the young girl tripped over and dropping the child. He ran off into the crowd once he got to his feet. The young girl was handed back to Sue, crying and all upset over the ordeal. They informed the police, who suggested Sue doesn't go out without being accompanied by one of them or a security guard.

The next day, Sue stayed home, and a courier came to her home delivering a parcel. She thought it suspicious that a parcel would be delivered to her on a Sunday, so she rang the police, who came around and began examining the parcel. After carefully taking the wrapping off, they could see some wires in the box and called for the bomb squad.

The bomb squad took the parcel to a remote area and used a robot to unpack the parcel. After opening the box, they tipped it over to reveal it was a makeshift bomb, but it was not activated. It was meant to scare Sue and not blow her up.

The police took Sue and the children to a secure house and placed a guard at the front door to insure no one would break in to damage the property.

Tim Hoe was another witness who will swear an affidavit as to what had happened to him and his family in Hong Kong. He was on his way to work, just walking up the stairs of the subway, when he was stabbed from behind and fell to the ground bleeding from a knife wound in the back. An ambulance was called, and they rushed him to the hospital in a critical condition. He had lost a lot of blood and underwent an emergency operation to repair the severed artery. His wife was called to the hospital, and she was waiting in the waiting room as they wheeled him out of the operating theatre. The doctor came out to tell her they repaired the damage, and he would make a full recovery. After a week in hospital, Tim withdrew from the proceedings as his wife had been threatened and they did not believe the police could adequately protect them.

Another witness, Julie Woy, also received a threatening phone call, but she refused to be intimidated. One night as the family sat in the lounge room watching television, a bottle was thrown through the window with one end alight. Julie quickly picked up the bottle and ran to the front door. She could see a blue BMW parked in the street with a man in the driver's seat and the other just getting into the car.

She threw the bottle at the car and got it, landing on the back seat as the window had been wound down. The Molotov cocktail exploded, and both men leapt out of the vehicle as it was engulfed in flames.

One man walked towards Julie, and she could see he had a gun under his coat. As he neared her, sirens sounded, and two police cars came out of nowhere. The police immediately rushed towards the car and then, seeing the driver approach, Julie went after him. The driver stopped in his tracks and was ready to turn around and walk away when the police grabbed him and asked him some questions. They noticed he had a gun and immediately took this from him.

The man refused to answer questions and declared immunity as he was a member of the Chinese Consulate. They took the man into custody for questioning, but he refused to answer questions put to him.

Julie told the police what had happened and after the fire brigade put the fire out, they made a search of the car, which revealed several documents naming other witnesses, which were also marked for the same treatment.

The FBI were called in and, after much deliberation, placed all of those who swore an affidavit under protection. They released the man arrested on bail, but he never appeared in court with his record eventually marked "whereabouts unknown."

CHAPTER 28

The President woke up the next morning after staying at the hospital that night. He was given breakfast and his staff brought him clean clothes to wear. He showered and prepared himself for the long flight to the Eastern Province. He sat back in a chair in his room listing to the news, which was mostly about the rain and the damage it had caused.

He closed his eyes but still listening to the news, hearing rivers had broken their banks and flooded many areas and townships that have never seen floods before. He heard many villagers had been swept away in the fast-moving rivers that had inundated their homes and livestock could not be saved and were swept to their death as the water was deep and fast moving. His concentration was interrupted by the sound of a helicopter landing close by and knew his journey would soon begin.

An officer appeared at the President's door who introduced himself and advised they were ready to make the trip to the Eastern Province. The President thanked the doctors and nurses for looking after him and told the officer to lead the way to the helicopter.

Five minutes later, the President was airborne. He could see the devastation that had been done to the countryside, and that water lay everywhere, with many villages totally flooded. All that could be seen was the tips of the roof of their houses protruding from the flood. Many had lost all their possessions.

After flying over the water for an hour, the group came in sight of an area that was not flooded and beneath could be seen fields of crops being harvested and herds of sheep and cattle grazing in lush paddocks. After flying over this for about thirty minutes, the helicopters landed in a field and the engines were switched off. The soldiers lined up and moved to the community hall, followed by the President.

When they arrived, the head of the Peoples Committee warmly welcomed the President to their village and ushered him into the community building where the villagers were waiting to greet him.

The head of the village said, 'Mr President, welcome to our village. May we arrange for some tea for you and your entourage?'

The President said, 'Thank you. I appreciate your warm welcome.'

They all had tea, including the soldiers that accompanied the President, after which they moved to a private room as the President was eager to discuss what he had seen. The President requested the Monk join them, and since he was not present. He was summoned.

After a few minutes, the Monk appeared and greeted the President and sat down.

The President said, 'I am sure you expected us to visit your village as you predicted the endless fall of rain. We now wish to have this stopped and believe this is in your power to do this.'

The Monk said, 'No we had nothing to do with the rain. You wanted to bomb our village and our church and refused to acknowledge our God or allow religion to exist. In fact, you wanted all of China to bow before you as God, and you were not allowing freedom of worship. Our God advised you this would happen to show you that you are nothing but a man trying to elevate yourself to the position of a god. Our God would not allow you to do this and therefore has caused the rain to fall so you can judge who is the greater you or your creator.'

The President said, 'I will not enter an argument with you. But this rain must stop, and I hold you responsible for the flooding and misfortune that has fallen upon our nation.'

The Monk said, 'You are the one responsible, not us. We did not make ourselves out to be gods. You did this, not us. Your Congress supported you and therefore the rains came as I predicted and declared by our lord.'

The President said, 'You must stop the rains. I do not care who is responsible, but the rain must stop. If you do not stop the rain, I will put a bullet in you.'

With that, the President grabbed the pistol from the nearest soldier's belt and pointed it at the Monk. The villagers present immediately rose to their feet and surrounded the Monk to prevent him from being shot.

The Monk moved away from the villagers, signalling for them to resume their seats. He walked up to the President and said, 'If you intend to shoot me, then do so as I nor any of my fellow villagers have caused the rain. It is God that controls this, not us. Yet after so many things that have happened, you still will not believe in God or ask him for help. You come here to threaten us with death if we refuse to follow your orders. You say you are a god, then stop the rain from falling. Your powers should enable you to do this. You can't because you are nothing but a man in sheep's clothing.'

With that, the President aimed the gun at the Monk and squeezed the trigger. The gun went off and everyone looked at the Monk, expecting him to fall to the ground. Instead, he stood upright looking at the President who by this time had dropped the gun and was grasping his hand, which had blood gashing out from open wounds. The gun had blown up in the President's hand. The soldiers close to the President grabbed hold of his hand and could see that the gun had jammed backfiring as if the President had a grenade exploding in the palm of his hand. One soldier ran to the helicopter to grab the first aid kit.

The monk grabbed the scarf he was wearing and moved closer to the President intending to bandage the President's hand. As he moved towards the President, a soldier pulled out his gun and aimed it towards the Monk's heart. He pulled the trigger. The Monk fell to the ground.

The President moved to where the Monk laid and rolled the body over, expecting the worst to see a gashing wound but could see no injury. He felt around the Monk's chest, but there was nothing, no hole and no bullet. The Monk had nothing on as body protection, or a bullet proof garment. All that he had on was the Monk's robes and a long outer scarf.

As the President was looking over the body, the Monk came too and, upon seeing the President leaning over him, immediately, to the surprise of all those present, got to his feet.

The President was speechless and immediately ordered the soldier to put his gun away and not to use it again.

The Monk moved towards the President, holding his scarf in his hands, and the same soldier again pulled his gun and aimed it towards the monk, despite being ordered not to take his gun out of his holster. With this, the President grabbed a revolver from the belt of a soldier standing near him, aimed it directly at the soldier's head and pulled the trigger, hitting the soldier in the forehead. The soldier turned slightly staring at the President momentarily and then fell to the ground, bleeding profusely from his wound. The President ordered the body be taken out and put the gun back in the soldier's holster from where he took it.

The President moved towards the Monk and said, 'How can you still be alive? You were shot at close range, so the soldier could not have missed you. He aimed the gun directly at your heart. If he missed, he still would have hit your chest, but you have sustained no injury. This is impossible?'

The Monk replied, 'All things are possible to our Lord. You are looking at things the way a normal mortal would rather than from the view that nothing is impossible for our Lord. He no doubt wanted to show you what he can do and has allowed the bullet to pass through me or he stopped it from entering my body. Have you checked the wall behind me to see if the bullet entered the wall?'

President, looking bewildered, said, 'No, but I will have my soldiers do that right now.'

The President signalled for the officer in charge to check the wall and after a few minutes, the officer looked at the President and shook his head, showing nothing had been found.

The President could not understand what he had seen and momentarily lost his line of thinking, sitting down to think what had happened.

The Monk moved towards the President and wrapped his scarf around the President's hand, which was still in part, bleeding.

A soldier gave the President a bottle of water, which he drank half still trying to digest what had happened.

After a short time, he decided to go back to headquarters and try to think about what had happened and try to come up with a logical explanation. He signalled to his men that they will depart and gave the order to move back to the helicopters. He thanked the leader of the Peoples Committee for their attendance and support and advised he would be back to resume his discussions with the Committee and the monk. One soldier opened the medical kit he got from the helicopter and removed the Monk's scarf from the hand of the president. He applied what seemed to be an antiseptic from a spray can and bandaged the president's hand. He gave the scarf back to the Monk. With that, the President ordered his men back to the helicopters.

The President was in extreme pain and could barely talk. He hurried to the helicopter and sat down in it as the propellers picked up speed and they took off.

The monk and all the villagers all were speechless as to what had happened and they moved to the church to thank God for protecting them and to ask for the rain to stop to allow what crops were not damaged, to be harvested.

That night in a dream the Monk received a message that the Lord would not yet stop the rain as he will not be considered either a puppet of the President nor allow the President to think he is a God as Satin was manipulating the President and wanted the world to think the President was a god and should be worshipped. Eventually, Satin would eliminate the President and take his place once the world worshipped the President.

The President was to act as if he was in control while he was being manipulated by Satin for world dominance. His country had more population than any other country in the world and was building up its military might to ensure no one would challenge it.

The President was taken immediately to the Beijing hospital and was taken into the operating theatre for a reconstruction of his hand.

He stayed in hospital for a week and was released with physiotherapy treatment thereafter to get the hand to move naturally.

The President immediately called a meeting of the National People's Committee to advise them of what had happened at the Eastern Province and to address the flooding being experienced nationwide.

The meeting was fiery, with most delegates insisting on the Monk being brought before them to explain why he refused to stop the rain. The President explained what had happened and that the Monk insisted he had nothing to do with the rain and could not stop it. It was his God that controlled the rain and not the Monk.

The delegates refused to accept this line of thinking and insisted on the Monk being brought before them and the members of the National People's Committee. It was agreed that a military operation would be immediately sent to the region to bring back the Monk and the Committee members and that the Peoples Committee was to reconvene the next day to question the Monk and his Committee.

Twenty men were designated to go in three helicopters to bring the Monk and the Committee members back. They took off immediately upon receiving their orders.

After flying for an hour, they finally reached the Eastern Province and landed in the oval near the church. They immediately entered the village and went to the main hall to arrest the Committee members and the Monk. No one was in the hall, so they had to go from village to village to find the people required to be brought back to Beijing. Eventually, after several hours had passed, they got the people they were looking for and bundled them up into the helicopters for the return journey. Once they landed, they took everyone to the jail and locked them up, so they did not escape. The next morning, all were given a very brief breakfast and taken to the main hall to appear before the National People's Committee.

The delegates took care of procedural matters for an hour before the Monk and Committee members were brought in to face the National People's Committee.

The President sat in the assembly but did not take control, leaving this to the Speaker of the House, who addressed the meeting as soon as the Monk and Committee members were brought in. He advised the house that these men were brought in as they refused to co-operate with the National People's Committee and stop the rain, which was causing enormous flooding nationwide.

The men stood there while they were being criticised and warned what would happen to them if they did not co-operate and stopped the rain.

The Monk stood up and advised the Committee that they have nothing to do with the rain and that it was an act of God owing to the decision taken by the President to declare himself a God of the People and the Committee agreeing with him. The Monk said, 'If you are a God, then stop the rain. Otherwise, you are only a fool who is trying to challenge our Lord and in doing so will suffer the consequences.'

The Speaker stood up and said, 'You will either stop the rain or each of you will be shot to show we will not tolerate your God or your foolishness. Stop it now or the guards can take you out one by one and shoot you now.'

The Monk was sitting down, and the Lord spoke to him. After a minute he stood up and looked at the National People's Committee and said, 'I believe that not all the Committee agree with your proposal to shoot us. Let there be a show of hands by those who agree with the Speaker's decision.'

Slowly, hands were being raised with eventually about a hundred hands pointed upwards. The Speaker was surprised, as he thought he would have more support than this.

The Monk then stood up and said, 'You who have agreed with the Speaker shall receive from God the same judgement that has been imposed on us, for you have challenged the Lord. The judgement shall be the same as you intended for us, except your life will end at the hands of the Lord. As the clock in the great hall chimes midday, you will die. Every one of you who opposed our Lord.' With that, the Monk sat down.

The Speaker stood up and with a smear on his face said, 'You will not scare us. The clock has but five minutes before it chimes, and do you think we believe in this foolishness? We will decide what happens to you and not the other way around. Stop the rain or we will take you out and shoot you.'

The Monk could see the clock arm had reached twelve o'clock and chimed. All the members looked at the clock with some standing to see the time. Nothing happened until the chimes stopped. Everyone then looked at where the Speaker stood but could not see him. They then glanced at the other members that were standing, but none could be seen until it was noted they were face down on the floor. Upon further investigation, it was found that they were not breathing, and a doctor was called to examine them.

The doctor arrived within a minute and examined the bodies, declaring them one by one as dead.

The House went into an uproar with members streaming out of the building for fear that they may also be struck down, as were their colleagues.

The President, who did not take part in the proceedings, got up and ordered the soldiers to arrest the Monk and the Committee members and to hold them under House arrest in jail. This was done, and the bodies removed from the House. After an hour, the members moved back into the assembly and sat quietly until the President rose to speak. He said, 'You have all seen with your own eyes the power of the Monks God. I experienced it when I went to the Eastern Province, as I had explained to you. Those who want their blood please stand. Not a person stood up. We will now bring the Eastern Province men back into the chamber as we need to stop the rain, as we have lost most of our crops and quite a few villages.'

After assembling, the President addressed the group, asking about their God's intentions to end the rain. The President said, 'Our people have had enough, and it is causing a wide spread of destruction and loss of life, both in animal stock and humans.'

The Monk stood up and began nervously to address the Congress, saying, 'You have tried to present yourselves as Gods thinking you have the power our Lord has. He has shown you he is in charge and not you. It is His world. He created it and not you whom he has allowed the right to live and bread. You dare to take your greatness to the point of threatening his church by outlawing the assembly of worshipers. Let it be made clear that the right of religion has been given to man from God and the State shall never have the right to stop this. You are not

Gods but men thinking you can challenge the maker. The Lord has shown you what he can do. Remember this. From midnight tonight, the rain will stop, and the waters allowed to recede. So says the Lord.' The monk then sat down.

The assembly went into an uproar until the members quietened down and began talking amongst themselves. The President then stood up and declared the meeting closed. Some members didn't think the Monk deserved to live because they held him responsible for the deaths and the rain. Not an invisible God, but they would not stand their ground and insist on it. In their eyes, there will be plenty of time to settle the score later down the track. All moved out of the building in an orderly fashion, leaving the Monk and the Committee members still sitting in the chamber. They were waiting for the authorities to come and again lock them up, but no one came, so they moved out of the building.

The rain was still pouring down, causing flooding and debris to wash past them, making it impossible for them to walk anywhere. They moved back into the Assembly and ended up in the kitchen where they noted there were fridges of food and gas cookers for commercial use. They had no food since taken from their village and were starving.

They took from the fridges what they needed as meat and vegetables and made themselves various dishes to eat. They gave thanks to the Lord for the food He graciously provided them with. The food they had cooked was supported by some wine that they found and fruit.

After they had completed their meal, they washed up as best they could and went to the back of the building onto a covered veranda that was enclosed. They took cushions from chairs that were there and made beds and settled down and went to sleep. They slept until shortly past midnight when they woke up and noted the rain had stopped as the Lord had said it would. The flooding was still present, so they waited a couple of hours before heading off. They slept on until dawn and went back into the kitchen to have breakfast, as they knew the day would be a long one.

After a quick breakfast, they went into the street and could see the damage done to the roads, bridges, and buildings. They walked for about an hour on what seemed an endless journey leading to nowhere, however they kept ongoing. Eventually, they arrived at a large truck depot and began walking through it. They could see that the vehicles had been parked in haste, as they were not evenly spaced and skewed and not within parking bays, but across them.

The Monk looked into the trucks they walked past and could see that the keys were left in the vehicles, as had been previously the case. He tried to start some of them, but they would not turn over. He continually looked into the cabin of the vehicle and then tries to start it. Eventually, one started, and they all piled into the back as the monk maneuvered the truck around the yard and onto the road. He went slowly as there was a lot of debris on the road and he did not want to hit any of it.

After driving a few hours, the road opened and was not as difficult as before in trying to avoid obstacles. They took turns in driving and after travelling twenty hours arrived home to the amazement of the villagers.

That the villages were informed that the rain had stopped falling, but a lot of the damage to homes and crops could not be prevented or rectified. Many will have to start afresh, which was not possible as materials were scarce for rebuilding and seed and fertiliser was costly as the Government had made many enemies in both Europe, Australia and in America.

The President appeared on national television with his hand bandaged, declaring he could stop the rain, and was negotiating with other countries to provide welfare and grain to China. He declared the rain was an abnormal event associated with climate change and the warming of the planet. He refused to tell the nation the truth and said nothing further about banning religion.

CHAPTER 29

The President (of China) called to his office the head of the secret service to find out the situation what they have done about Sue and those involved in the case brought before the International Human Rights Commission. He paced up and down his office, reading a report from his legal advisers about what they should do about the case. He was not happy about their conclusion, which declared they should attend and defend the action.

He knew if allowed, the truth would make him and China the laughingstock of the world. The only way China had in the past gained respect was by force using both economic and military force to get its way. He did not intend to change now.

His secretary interrupted him, advising that the head of the secret service was on his way to his office. As they were speaking, the head came into the President's office and was shown a seat. The door was closed, and both men talked.

President said, 'Why are those witnesses still alive? I told you to get rid of them. We do not want the embarrassment of being found to have acted against human rights, even though those we have dealt with deserved what they got.'

Head of Secret Service said, 'We cannot get near the witnesses or their families as they are being protected by the police.'

President said, 'Then buy the police off. Do whatever you have to do to kill every one of those who has acted against us. I want this ended.'

Head of Secret Service said, 'We will do our best.'

President said, 'Your best has not been good enough so far. If you fail, you will be replaced with someone who can do the job.'

With that, the President walked out of the room, leaving the Head of Secret Service sitting in his chair momentarily, not understanding what they had said. When it did dawn upon him, he understood professional assassins would need to be hired to get ride off all those that opposed the Peoples Republic of China.

He walked out of the office to arrange for a hit squad to do the job, as he was not prepared to give up his position or surrender the lives of his family.

Over the next few days, they selected three men to carry out the assassinations. They were given diplomatic passports, and their rifles would be given to them once they arrived in America. They would bring their rifles and ammunition into America in pieces in consulate bags which are not checked by Boarder Control.

Each of the assassins would receive a set fee to kill those named on their list.

CHAPTER 30

The assassins had no trouble in getting into the country on diplomatic passports. The first assassin's assignment was to kill one of the outspoken leaders of the Hong Kong movement, that was allowed entry into America and had been given residency there. The second assassin was to take care of Sue, while the third was to kill as many of the witnesses that had agreed to give evidence at the Human Rights Commission.

The outspoken leader was Adrian Tu, who soon became a recognised name in America and very outspoken against the Chinese government. Adrian became a reputable reporter through hard work after learning his trade in Hong Kong. He left just before China's takeover.

Adrian not only had a television show in a popular time slot but also wrote a column in the local Journal which was recognised as the leading source of news and events. He had a wife and two children and had brought over his parents and his wife's parents with him to ensure the Chinese would not arrest them on fictitious charges.

He became a real thorn in the side of the Chinese Government as he seemed to get insider tips as to what Beijing was about to do and could support his accusations with evidence. The Chines government knew it could not stop the leaks but decided to stop him reporting. This would then give a clear indication to others that they were not safe, no matter where they were located.

Adrian arranged for a televised interview with Sue to bring his listeners up to date as to what was happening in Sue's Human Rights case. The venue was outdoors in a park.

Sue arrived and walked up to the production crew. Adrian, who was in one of the caravans, saw her, came out and walked up to her. As he did this, a gust of wind blew over a large A frame that was being used as a backdrop. As the frame was leaning partially over before being blown over, it covered Adrian's body. A shot rang out and Adrian fell to the ground, bleeding from the head, while the frame fell on top of him.

The production team, who heard the sound, looked at Adrian, who was lying on the ground, and ran up to him. They noticed blood coming from a head wound and immediately called for an ambulance.

The paramedics arrived within minutes of the call being made and concluded that the graze was made by a bullet and called the police to report what they believed to be an attempt on Adrian's life.

The police arrived within minutes of receiving the call and agreed with the findings of the paramedics. They believed the frame distracted the shooter and was the factor saving Adrian's life. The bullet was located and proved that it came from a sniper's rifle.

Sue stood back to allow the police to do their search of the area and dig up the bullet. As she stood waiting to see what had happened to Adrian, another shot rang out. The policeman standing near Sue pulled her to the ground just as a bullet landed in the notice board behind them. Sue, realising she was being shot at, ran to a nearby police car and crouched down so the shooter could not see her.

The police immediately called in a helicopter to see from which roof top the shooter was on. After a few minutes flying around, the chopper could locate a person on the roof of a multistorey building and that he had a rifle. The shooter, seeing the helicopter, raised his rifle and shot at the helicopter, breaking the windscreen. He shot again, but this time the bullet hit the seat in the helicopter, forcing it to move away from the building.

Police surrounded the building and with guns drawn, went onto the roof where they thought the shooter would be located. They found the rifle, but the shooter had escaped. They did not believe he had left the building but was hiding on one floor as a worker. Sniffer dogs were brought in, and the police went from floor to floor trying to find the shooter. They believed that the person would have a sense of gunpowder on their hands and the dog could sniff this out. Unfortunately, the dog could not point out the person.

As Sue was being escorted out of the building, a man tried to grab her so he could stab her, but instead stabbed one of the policemen in the shoulder. For a moment, no one knew what had happened until the policeman drew his gun and shot at the person who had stabbed him. Everyone froze as the policeman dropped his gun to pull the knife out of his shoulder. Sue screamed, and the policeman collapsed in a half-crouched position, grabbing his shoulder. Other policemen standing nearby ran to help him. The assassin, who was not injured, ran off as if he was trying to get out of danger. The policeman yelled out for others to stop the person from running off, but it was too late, as the assassin had already made his escape. The policeman was rushed to hospital and immediately underwent an operation to stop the bleeding.

Sue was taken home with specific instructions not to go out without a police escort.

About an hour afterwards, Sue receives a visit from Adrian and his crew, who set up their equipment in her lounge room. Adrian was determined to have his interview so he could broadcast it that evening.

The interview went well, and Sue could describe what had happened with her case before the Human Rights Commission and China's attempt to stop it. She also brought up the attempt to silence her and some witnesses. She recounted the number that had been killed and the attempt to blackmail others by imprisoning their relatives who were back in China. Additionally, she recounted today's events and emphasised that these were not isolated incidents, but a deliberate attempt by China to silence their critics.

The interview ended, and the crew packed up and waited for Adrian, who was discussing some issues raised in the course of the interview. The crew was getting anxious, so two of the men went back into the house to see what the holdup was. As they opened the front door, the television van in the driveway exploded as if it had been bombed and burst into flames which engulfed it completely. No one could escape as it happened too quickly, and they would have been killed either by the blast or the fire. Sue and Adrian, who were near the front door, could only look on as the van while it burnt. Eventually, the fire brigade extinguished the fire. The police arrived soon afterwards and could ascertain that a military rocket had been fired at the van, causing it to explode. The rocket was shot from a passing car. No doubt the next attempt will be at Sue and the house.

Adrian and the remaining crew members got a lift from the police and went back to their office to prepare for the show. They had lost two of their fellow workers, plus the equipment used to do mobile interviews. The program started with Adrian declaring what had happened and advised that he believed the Chinese Government was behind the plots and deaths of his colleagues. He was able to get pictures of the three assassins that came into the country as diplomats that were behind the attempt to kill him and who had killed his crew and showed this on his show broadcasting their image across America.

The Chinese Government denied having anything to do with the killings or being involved, even though the three came into the country on diplomatic passports.

A few days later, the three men were discovered in a shipping container dead with bullet holes in their foreheads.

Sue continued on with the application to the Human Rights Commission, always looking over her shoulder to ensure no one was there ready to put a knife into her or worst, do something to her children.

CHAPTER 31

The Chinese economy was faulting, and the President knew he could not make many more poor decisions if he wanted to remain in power. China had planned a meeting with Russia to discuss strategic, military, and economic development just when China's reserves were low. The Chinese delegation was briefed what it wanted from Russia and what it believed Russia wanted from China.

The meeting was scheduled to take place in Moscow and all protocols were in place to greet the Chinese President and his entourage. Security was tight, and there were more police and military on the ground than diplomats.

The meeting started with the Russian President (RP), welcoming all to the meeting and allowed thirty minutes for photographs and reporters to ask pre-planned questions of the Chinese President (CP). After they completed the formalities, the Russian president invited the Chinese President to his private office so they could have a one-on-one discussion. This was not part of the plan agreed to by the Chinese President, but he went along with the request as he was inquisitive as to what the Russians wanted.

RP said, 'I have asked you here so I can speak to you about what had happened in Hong Kong and why you did not send in soldiers immediately when the uprising occurred."

CP said, 'We do not believe our handling of Hong Kong has anything to do with you or any bearing on this round of discussions between our two nations.'

RP said, 'No it hasn't, but I would be very interested to know as we have a similar situation which we intend to force and I would like to get an idea of what reaction you got from the other countries, particular from NATO countries.'

CP said, 'We made sure that we took all avenues for peaceful settlement first before making our demands clear to the population of Hong Kong and before using force. Why, who do you intend to attack?'

RP said, 'Ukraine.'

CP said, 'You will have the entire world against you.'

RP said, 'They will condemn us but do nothing. It will be like Hitler rolling into Poland. A lot of talk and promises, with little action. The American do not want another war to get involved in so they will talk a lot but do nothing.'

CP said, 'You hope. They may decide to change their position and get involved, which will mean Russia against the world.'

RP said, 'You will surely come to our aid and help defend us?'

CP said, 'We will have our own battles to fight in Hong Kong and Taiwan and therefore cannot guarantee to support you. Also, we may decide China should take world dominance and not share our might and greatness with another country.'

RP said, 'We noted that America and England made a lot of noise about democracy and people's rights when you sent in the army to establish law and order but did little to assist the people except show pictures of arrests in the evening news. We think the same situation will occur when we make our move towards Ukraine. We will be ready to stretch it out diplomatically and may veto any resolutions that the west may try to put through the United Nations.'

CP said, 'We will look how you go with your effort to gain Ukraine territory before making any move on Taiwan. We do not need support from any nation, as we have built our military up over the last decade and we are strong, with a lot of trained men and a contingent of warships and submarines.'

We have been buying Australian iron ore to make steel over many years on the pretext that we were expanding our economy and establishing new major cities for our population to move into, but in reality, we have been building up our fleet of destroyers, carriers, and submarines. The number of vessels we have now exceeds what America holds in military equipment and we can destroy anyone who dares to challenge us.'

RP said, 'Therefore I want your support should things go wrong as we know you have a greater capability to destroy America should they move on you. Also, with you by our side, America will not move against us and support Ukraine.'

CP said, 'We are prepared to support you in the United Nations, but not militarily. We will need all our equipment and men to fight our own wars, which could happen if America does not refrain from supporting Taiwan.'

RP said, 'This meeting is to be kept secret, between us only. I know I can rely on you to tell no one.'

The two men left the meeting to join the other members, who were discussing a free trade agreement.

CHAPTER 32

The Prime mister of Taiwan called a meeting of Congress to discuss emergency measures should China attack his country. On the agenda were reports from their Bureau of Internal Affairs, which believes China will attach Taiwan to annex its territory to be part of China within the next year. The report highlights China's intention to secure industry, which Taiwan has, and China wants, because of their critical importance to world trade and communications. Amongst many items produced out of Taiwan are computer chips, which are one of the main crucial products for computers, scientific equipment, manufacturing machinery, automobiles, just to name a few. Also, Taiwan produces leading medical equipment and telescopes for scientific work and exploration.

Amongst the recommendations for consideration was a proposal to sell or lease some of these industries off to other friendly countries, on either an outright basis or on a royalty basis.

Congress discusses the proposals over three days agreeing to approach two countries to see if they would be interested in acquiring the patent rights to the products manufactured or come up with another suggestion to ensure China did not gain the knowledge or control of manufacturing the products. The two countries nominated were Australia and Israel.

Congress agreed to establish a working party of five members who would seek discussions with each nominated country and report back to congress within ninety days. To keep their intentions secret, they agreed to declare that Taiwan's Congress had agreed to hold preliminary talks with countries to see if they could secure a Free Trade Agreement. This would legitimise the movement of personnel and working groups between countries and not appear unusual or concerning.

They established formal lines of communications between the countries and agriculture and raw materials were the first item on the agenda. Meetings were established in each country and a small group established to spearhead the discussions and come back to the Congress once these had been concluded.

A week before departure to Australia, the Prime minister of Taiwan telephoned the prime minister of Australia requesting a private meeting so security issues could be discussed and recommended that the Minister of Defence and ASIO be present so frank talks could take place. The meeting was scheduled, and briefing notes sent to Australia in relations to the agenda of the free trade meetings.

A week had passed, and the Taiwanese were greeted by the Australian Prime Minister who held a press conference to explain why they were in Australia and that it was hoped that this would be the first of many meetings to establish a free trade agreement between the countries covering many fronts. The initial meetings were to find out the areas that were of primary concern and of interest to each country, and to see what issues would prevent a free trade of these industries or commodities.

The Prime Minister deputised the minister for trade to control the negotiation and to ensure the meetings were productive. They had established a working party by the Prime Minister and the first item on the agenda was to establish the areas where a free trade agreement would benefit both countries, strategically and economically. While they held the preliminary meetings, they arranged a private meeting between the two country's Prime Ministers.

The Taiwanese Prime Minister took the initiative at that meeting declaring the purpose of the private meeting and that they feared invasion from China, which would be sooner than later. At the meeting were the head of ASIO and defence personnel.

As the meeting progressed, Australia showed interest in taking some of the manufacturing industries over that were established in Taiwan, but was concerned with what China would do once it found out. They agreed the plan required a broader involvement before they could agree, as Australia could not defend itself against China's military might. They agreed they would invite in America and England to take part in the free trade agreements on the pretext that they wanted to establish a Pacific involvement in the area.

The two countries were formally invited to take part and would send a negotiating committee to represent them. Both countries were very keen to be involved in talks regards the transfer of major industries to Australia or one of the other countries represented at the meeting. They agreed China would not attack England or America as they were part of the NATO alliance who could match China military might should they try to cause trouble. They agreed China would not allow Taiwan's industries to re-establish themselves in any of the European countries or America. However, Australia, because of its small population and being poorly equipped militarily, may not cause China concern.

They agreed over many months of negotiation that they could establish a reasonable enough argument whereby Taiwan agrees to move its manufacturing industries, that are affected by shipping, to Australia and manufacture in Australia rather than importing the raw materials to Taiwan and manufacturing from that country. Shipping costs were becoming a major overhead that soon would bankrupt the country if allowed to continue coupled with supply chain problems experienced by Covid-19 and the pandemic. Also, the Chinese blockade of the international waters near China made shipping precarious.

Australia agreed to allow Taiwan to establish its industries in Australia and receive royalties on goods manufactured and sold overseas. It would allow the transfer of Taiwanese skilled workers to come to Australia on a separate visa and if they decided they could become Australian citizens after five years of residency.

They agreed Taiwan would establish a boat building industry in Australia to help it build up its naval fleet and establishing a base for its nuclear submarines. It would also assist in the establishment of a chip manufacturing industry in Australia to manufacture the older style chips, while Taiwan would concentrate on manufacturing more advanced chips for the military and scientific equipment.

Similar meetings were held in Israel however while they could provide more security from a military point of view the culture and customs of the two countries were different to the degree that Taiwan citizens would not move permanently to Israel nor be part of that country's laws relating to subscription into the army once a person turned eighteen.

America had military treaties with Taiwan and Australia, agreed it would be only a matter of time before China made its move militarily to gain Taiwan and take over the country. When that happens, it will not be possible to move personnel and industry out of Taiwan.

England was very interested in establishing a free trade agreement with Taiwan and took part in the negotiations. It was also interested in entering a manufacturing agreement with Taiwan to supply some components to them or to the relocated industries in Australia. This would make it harder for China to take over all of Taiwan's manufacture should they invade Taiwan.

America had already made agreements with Taiwan and did not need to renegotiate its position. However, America was very keen to have the chip and scientific areas transferred to Australia to make sure China did not gain access to the technology, which it assumed it would once it invaded Taiwan.

Australia and Taiwan made a licensing agreement for computer chip manufacturing. They built a plant in Melbourne and hired skilled Taiwanese workers over a period of four months. Workers could come to Australia with their families and were assisted by housing and schooling for their children. After five years, they could become Australian citizens if they desired, or return home depending upon the threat imposed by China.

To this, a boatbuilding industry was established in Sydney and the one in South Australia was expanded to take larger vessels and submarines. Strategically, it was felt that South Australia would be more secure from a security point of view than Sydney from rocket attacks and possibly an invasion.

America supported these moves and assisted in the funding the process. Over time, the Taiwanese licenced more and more industries to manufacture products in Australia and more Taiwanese citizens took up the offer to move to Australia as it was becoming apparent that China intended to take over Taiwan.

Australia built up its manufacturing industry and became less reliant on overseas suppliers of components and equipment. The country moved to a position of becoming self-sufficient to ensure it could stifle any move to cripple its industry should China increase its aggressiveness in the south seas.

America increased its emphasis on encouraging industry that had established a manufacturing base in Taiwan and or China to move themselves back to American shores. They encouraged these industries through tariff and tax incentives. Over time, many industries moved back to America as politically it was becoming obvious that China was going to exert military dominance in the world.

CHAPTER 33

Sue sat in her study, trying to concentrate on drafting an additional document the International Human Rights Commission requested. She noted she was once again staring into a black hole of nothing, trying to get the fog out of her mind. She realised she was again slipping back into depression and would need to avoid this at all costs.

She drafted her affidavit and just when she completed it, received a phone call from her sister, who went to collect the kids from school. She advised Sue that the school let the kids go with someone who said she was a friend of Sues who took the kids to a car and drove off with them.

Sue became very upset, as she knew something was wrong and that the kids were in danger. She immediately called Jerry, who called the police, and they came immediately to Sue's house. They sent a car to the school to see if anyone had seen anything, but no one knew a thing. They spoke to Sue's sister Irene, who was staying with Sue after her husband had died some months ago of cancer. She had collected the kids every evening for the last two months as she was looking after the kids while Sue concentrated on her work.

Irene returned to Sue's house, not knowing what to say. The police did a door-to-door check of the neighbourhood and had the kid's photos shown on the news, hoping someone had seen them.

Sue was beside herself, thinking the worst would happen to the kids. She knew it would not be just a kidnapping. No, this one had a motive behind it and was sinister. She sensed Satin's hand was on the scheme to damage her and her family.

After about two days, Sue received a phone call from a man with a Chinese accent telling her she would not see her children again unless she withdraws her application to the International Human Rights Commission.

Sue immediately telephoned Jerry and advised him of the demand who intern, telephoned the police and advised them of the kidnapping.

Sue sat in a chair in her lounge room, thinking about the kidnapping. She thought she should have foreseen this would happen knowing what transpired in Hong Kong. She knew the Chinese were blood thirsty race of people and would not care about life or the life of her children. She decided to withdraw the application to the International Human Rights Commission because it was too dangerous and she couldn't find any trustworthy help, especially against China.

The police came to Sue's place wearing plan clothes as to not to tip off the kidnappers should they be close by watching the house. They came as a couple and greeted Sue as a friend, not letting on what the true reason was for them attending her house.

The police set up a recording base in Sues living room and brought in equipment so they could trace calls should another one was made.

Sue decided to go public on television, revealing that her children were kidnapped because China wanted her to withdraw her application with the International Human Rights Commission. She emphasised China wanted to sweep its history of human rights and in particular what occurred in Hong Kong, under the carpet. It did not want the world to know the truth. This was a risky tactic, but the police wanted the kidnappers to ring Sue again, so it was decided to aggravate them rather than appease them. The police believed the kidnappers were nearby Sues' house, monitoring her to make sure she did not do something that would embarrass the Chinese Government.

Sure enough, the kidnappers rang and advised they would kill her children if she spoke out again. Withdraw the application or she would not see her children again, ever.

After some time with the police, Sue went to her room to rest, as she was very upset and felt lonely without her children. She thought of God and as to why he would allow such miserable people to do what they have done to her children. What flashed into her mind was, 'Surely if there was a God, he would not allow this to happen.' They are only children and should be protected by God. The more she thought about it, the more she became angry towards God until she realised that Satin was putting these ideas in her mind. God would not allow this to happen, but would use this situation for the good of her cause.

Sue prayed to God for his understanding and asked for his help to get her children back uninjured. She acknowledged that this was no doubt a trial for her to see how much faith she really had in Jesus.

She sat in her room staring at the wall, not realising she was again drifting back into depression until she was disturbed by a knock at the door and a police officer brought in a MacDonalds and chips.

CHAPTER 34

I t was Sunday, and Sue was still without her children thinking the worst had happened to them. She knew she was getting depressed and decided to go to church as it had been a while since she attended a service. She advised the police about where she was going. One woman agreed to escort her to church.

Sue sat quietly in a pew, forth row from the front.

John Bishop stood up mid service and entered the pulpit. He hesitated for a moment, looking at his congregation, and noticed Sue was sitting close to the front and could see from her appearance she was not coping.

He began his sermon. 'Many of you here have had your problems with life. Most times, you find it is difficult, and it seems to get harder as time goes on. Why is God doing this to me must be the first thought going through your mind? Why does he make it so difficult, must be the second? What have I done to deserve this is no doubt the third? If there was a God, he would not allow this to happen, must be the fourth?'

'The reason things happen is privy to God, for you to ask him when you see him in heaven. Until then, trust His decision. Most times, none of us has an answer to the question. But sometimes, overtime, the answer is revealed to us.'

At this point some are already saying, 'Well that doesn't suit me.' And here lies the fork in the road. You either have faith declaring to

God you cannot understand his actions and how they have affected you. However, you will trust Him and would ask for his help to see why He has done what he has. Alternatively, you will walk away from Christ and seek your own course.'

'The Bible gives us a good look into God's reasoning and what could happen and why. Exodus is the chapter that shows clearly what God can do and why he does things his way and not yours.'

'There was a pharaoh, a leader of a mighty nation called Egypt who was to be taught a lesson. He would not let God's designated people go, so God taught him a lesson. Ten plagues were inflicted on his nation before he ordered the Jews out of Egypt, all one million of them.'

'Those that left Egypt were mainly practicing Jews and therefore knew of Yahweh and his promise of deliverance. Yet most had little faith, as in our time. They continually came up against life and death situations such as when they were all assembled at the Red Sea and Pharaoh's army came to kill them. Their backs were against the wall, with no avenue of escape from Pharaoh. Moses did not have the answer as to what to do, nor did those released from Egypt. But God had the answer. He ordered Moses to stretch out his stave across the sea and the waters opened, letting the mass to go forward. When Pharaoh tried to cross, the waters closed in on him and his army, killing most.'

'God puts you in a position where you cannot resolve a situation. Why? To prove to you that you do not have all the answers, but he does. This is why you should rely on Him in times of trouble. Most do not recognise they are being tested and think they are being punished or the trouble swamps them, and they do not know what to do, or declare the problem is too great for them to handle, and if there was a God, He would not have allowed this to happen.'

'The Israelites soon found themselves in a place once they cross the sea, where there was no water or food and instead of asking God what they should do, they complained again, criticising and declaring they had been let out of Egypt just to starve. After what God had done for them, you would think they would look towards Him for an answer. No, they looked at what they could produce, which amounted to nothing. They still had not learnt that God is in control, and they should look to Him for an answer and help. After a tense period, they were told that God would provide them with bread, meat to see them through their journey to the promise land and it happened just as God declared. He provided them with quail and manna.'

'You would have thought that after witnessing all these miracles, they would have learnt by now to rely on God, but not so. They wanted water. Where in the desert would you find drinking water? There was an oasis, but the water was undrinkable and again they complained and criticised God. Moses was told by God to throw a piece of wood that laid nearby into the oasis, and this made the water drinkable. A simple act that miraculously changed the water to allow his people to drink. Do you think they appreciated it? No, they still complained throughout the journey to where God had enough of them and declared they were not worthy to go to the promise land.'

'They walked the desert for forty years until the new generation came and were worthy with faith in God to do what he commanded.'

'What is the difference between these days and then? Only three thousand years. The situation is the same and only a handful of people truly believe in God and have the faith and trust in Him.'

'Let us pray....'

At the conclusion of the service, everyone stood up, but Sue had to wait to exit because the church was full, and people would take their time moving out.

John moved out of the pulpit and walked up to Sue and asked how she was. She turned to where he stood, looked at him, and burst into uncontrollable tears. He took her by the hand and led her to the front of the church, where he sat her down in one of the pews. After a minute, Sue told him about what had happed to her children and her fear that they were dead.

She then, after a few minutes, reflected on the service and the message John had conveyed in his sermon. She advised him she understood her children may already be dead, and that she expects the worse from the current situation. However, irrespective of what will come her way, she will have faith in God to see her through the dark periods and through her depression. Only he can manage this problem. It was out of her control. It was beyond her. She advised she regretted joining the Human Rights Commission team and wishes she could go back to being with her family.

John took Sue's hand and said a prayer. Both walked out of the church and went their separate ways.

CHAPTER 35

A policewoman called Sue after someone saw her on TV and reported seeing children in a house where there were none before. The caller suspected that nobody had moved in with a family because they hadn't seen any movers.

She advised the police she noticed the children being smacked as they tried to run from the people there. The curtains were rapidly closed to prevent anyone from seeing inside the room. An Asian man, who drew the curtains, hit a child, and an Asian woman caught her attention by holding a girl by both arms. The house had been vacant for some time until a few days ago, and she saw no one move in.

The police went to the women's house and talked to her, taking details of what she saw. The description she gave them matched the description of the children, which meant that they were still alive.

The police decided to create a diversion in the street to see if they could bring the occupants out of the house so they could see how many of them were there, while at the same time gain entry to the room where they thought the children were being held. They sourced some fireworks, and called on some teenagers in the street to let them off in front of the house while they gained entry from the rear window.

Sure enough, once the fireworks exploded, two men came out to see the kids letting them off. The police smashed the back window, opened it and moved inside the room, which was dark. The two children who were bound and in bed became visible as they shone their torches on them. They motioned to them to be quiet and cut the ropes binding their wrists. They then slid the children out of the window into the hands of other police officers who were waiting to take them away. Once clear, the police approached the front of the house, but no one opened the door. The SWAT team was brought in, and they smashed the front door down. The two men with guns in hand ran to the room where the children were bound to kill them, to ensure no witnesses existed before making their escape. The women had already run from the house as soon as the first lot of police knocked on the front door. She ran across the street where they had parked their car and was ready to drive off as soon as her two accomplices killed the children and joined her. To their surprise, the children were not in the room, so they tried to run down a hallway and get to the back door. As soon as they opened the backdoor, they were confronted by police who were waiting for them. One man aimed his gun at a policeman and was ready to shoot when another policeman opened fire, hitting the man in the arm sending his firearm flying to the ground, landing some distance from him. The other man dropped his weapon and put his hands up.

The men were taken back into the house and handcuffed. They were interrogated but refuse to answer questions. The police searched the house and found pictures of Sue and her sister in a folder and the words "eliminate if necessary" written under Sue's picture.

After about an hour, all the captives were led out of the house, handcuffed. As they approached the front gate, gunshots rang out and the two men laid faced down on the front lawn. All shot thorough the head by a sniper. The police immediately sought cover while those in the street tried to see where the shots came from. Since they could not pinpoint where the shooter was hiding, they stayed crouching behind cars in the street for some time. A minute later, another shot rang out, but no one could see where it came from.

After a few minutes, the police got up and moved to the area where they believe the shooter was held up, but he had already fled, leaving only empty gun shells.

The police went back to the house and as they approached it, they noticed a car in the street with a shattered windscreen. They moved towards it, thinking a strayed bullet did the damage. As they approached the car, they could see that there was a woman in the driver's seat with a bullet to the forehead. She was dead and assumed to be part of the team who kidnapped the children.

The police called in four body bags and began checking the house out to see what more they could find. There was a computer which showed the people had been paid a substantial amount to kidnap the children and notes found in the house suggested Sue was to be killed once she withdrew her application to the International Human Rights Commission.

The children were taken to the police station and given some milk and cookies to eat.

CHAPTER 36

A news flash came across the television as Sue looked up and then got out of her chair. She was in the lounge room and the news flash was that police had been involved in a shootout and two men were shot dead. She didn't relate this to her own problem until later she received a phone call from the police advising they had her children, and both were safe.

Sue immediately burst into tears and trembled and could not control her emotions and until a few minutes had passed. The children were put on the phone but could say nothing as they were traumatised and did not really understand what was happening. She was told that the children would be brought home shortly after they were able to tell police what had happened. Some three hours later, they arrived home, with Sue and the kids all bursting into tears as they greeted each other.

TV crews were waiting outside Sue's place; they broadcasted the entire event over national television and the scene was shown in many countries, including China. The president was not happy over the criticism laid against China and gave a news brief saying that his country had nothing to do with the kidnapping of the children or the death of the two men and women involved. The only problem was that the police never revealed how many men or woman were involved, yet the president could state accurately the number and their gender.

That night, after the kids were put to bed, Sue prayed to God, thanking Him for their safe return and forgiveness for her lack of faith in not trusting Him. After what she had been through, she could only think the worst would come from the kidnapping, and not the safe delivery of the children back to her. She asked God to help her understand why this happened and why she was put through the mental trauma.

She stood up and wondered, 'Why me Lord' and then remembered her previous decision to withdraw from the application to the International Human Rights Commission. Was this God's way of telling her he didn't want her to withdraw? She thought about it, then prayed to God to enlighten her as to what he wanted her to do, as this time it will be 'They will, will be done and not mine.'

Sue stayed home with the kids for a week, trying to settle them into their normal routine. A police presence was placed in the home to ensure no one would try to damage the premises or kill them. Two plainclothes policewomen were assigned to drop off and collect the children from school every day after the week.

Sue sat wondering what she should do, and decided the Lord wanted her to continue with the application against China in the International Human Rights Commission. Why would He force her to go through the troubles she experienced, if not to see it to the end? She was going to pull out, but the kidnapping of her children made her angry and who now was best equipped to tell the Commission about China. She would put her faith in Him and let Him Guide her, knowing she could be in no better hands. She went to the phone and phoned Jerry to discuss her intentions.

Jerry thought it was a bad idea, as no doubt the Chinese would have another go at her and the children to stop the application being lodged. There was little doubt the next time would not be a kidnapping, but to kill her. The conversation went around and around until it was agreed to speak to the police before deciding. A meeting was arranged for the next day in Jerry's office.

Sue turned up early and went to her desk to consider what was still to be done on the application. She was interrupted by Jerry, who phoned her. They were waiting for her to join them in Jerry's office.

Most were against the idea, but after discussing the application, it was agreed that Sue was the best person to attend to it. The next problem was what to do with the children and her safety.

It was agreed the children would stay with Sue's sister, Irene and a police presence would be there while Sue was working on the application. She would also have protection from a bodyguard hired by the firm to always stay with her while she was out of the office.

CHAPTER 37

Things have not gone well for the President, and he knows he must do something positive to change his image as he has come off second best in scheming to establish himself as a god of the people and the best man to ensure China's growth and success on the world stage.

He still wants to destroy the church in the Eastern Province and set himself up as God, eliminating all religion in China except the worship of him by the people. But the economy must come first and the destruction of farm produce by the rains has been costly. He thinks maybe there is a god who knows what he is thinking and will next time make sure he comes off even worse than he has.

He knows he must get agriculture moving again and therefore cannot risk upsetting the Monk's God, even though he believes he is a better god than the one the Monk prays to. At the back of his mind, he still believes the Monk is using 'Black Magic' as he doesn't believe in gods or a supernatural spirit, as often noted in the ancient mid-eastern writings. At least he can be seen and speak back or order your imprisonment if immediate death is not warranted. He knows that his position could change quickly if he doesn't perform or if the population learns the truth about the economy.

The President sits in his chair trying to come up with a way to establish wins for himself and silence his critics. He thinks, what he must do is stop looking within the country and concentrate on some external factor which would polarise the population's attention while he tries to clean up the mess internally.

He sits pondering over what he should do, and Satin moves his heart to towards world dominance, encouraging him to think he is a powerful, well-respected leader and no one would dare challenge him. Satin convinces the President that he must take an aggressive approach to winning back support and the best way was to take control of Taiwan.

After thinking about it, he decides to do something positive that will affect everyone in the country. He will call in his military chiefs to plan for the invasion of Taiwan. After this, he will tackle the church in the eastern province and expand China's dominance in other countries such as Africa, where he can take over the country economically and control their government. But then thinks why he should worry about war and control when I already control a third of the world's land mass and can control other counties economically. I am already a god without having to disturb the Monk's religion. Let him think about his god, which he can't see or hear. He will be the ruler in the future if he gets Taiwan and other countries in Africa and the Pacific. At least he is on this earth and can be seen and obeyed by those he commands and can show them what will happen should they not follow his orders.

He calls a meeting of the department heads of the military and advises them of his plan to invade Taiwan. He wants this to be kept secret, but they must come up with a plan as to how this will be achieved. The intention is to invade Taiwan and achieve control quickly, without allowing them to obstruct the invasion. It was agreed that the generals would consider the proposal and come back to him within two weeks to discuss their recommendation.

He makes it clear that they are to consider how this is to be achieved, not whether it should be done.

He also remembers that the International Human Rights Commission has requested assistance from the United Nations, who will meet in six weeks' time to vote on a motion against China's human rights abuses. He must veto this move by calling upon those countries who have borrowed money from China to vote in their favour and not against them.

He calls open his Foreign Affairs Department to go out to each of the governments they control, and ensure they vote against the UN motion.

The President knows the vote will be tight as the western countries, including America, will vote in favour of the motion.

The President recalls providing a substantial loan to an African country who recently gained voting rights in the UN. The country was broke when China moved in and established hospitals and a hydroelectric system to generate cheap power. This enabled industry to be established and the manufacturing of products cheaply. The country's economy flourished, and the population became educated. The only problem was that they were controlled by China and would be forced to vote as directed by China or their loans would have to be paid back immediately. Without money, the government did what China told them to do.

China ruled this country with a firm hand, as it did with other African counties whom it lent money to. They could expect at least six of the African countries to vote in China's favour.

The President did not like to play second fiddle to God and did not like the Monk in the eastern province to have the final say as to what was to happen in China. He thought about it and concluded that all religions in China were to cease, and that he was to be the only god to be worshipped. He would show the people his powers by destroying the church in the eastern province once and for all.

He called his generals into his office and advised them he wanted the church destroyed immediately, with no warning being given to the villagers. If the Monk was killed, then this would be to his advantage, as dead men do not speak the words of invisible gods. The complete plan was to be kept secret, so no one could tip the Monk off to ensure his God doesn't know what was to happen.

The Generals ordered two planes to bomb the church and gave the order to fuel up the plans and load them up with the bombs.

The bombs were loaded up first and afterwards, a fuel tanker ordered to fill the planes. As the tanker was approaching the planes, one technician was leaning over the instruments in the first plane and accidentally hit a switch which set one rocket off in a horizontal trajectory, which hit a large transport plane stationed some distance away. The plane blew up in a ball of fire which progressively spread to each of the planes parked nearby until it reached the tanker, which exploded, setting other planes on fire which had a bomb load attached. The planes exploded, demolishing the hanger in which they were in and some ten planes that were parked nearby. Some thirty-five planes were destroyed along with two refuelling tankers and two hangers.

The superior officers were immediately advised of what had happened.

The General responsible for that air force base sat quietly in his chair with the report on his desk which he had just finished reading. He pulled out his revolver from the drawer of his desk and looked at the pictures on his desk of his wife and children and put the gun to his stemple and squeezed the trigger.

The President was informed that the General lost his life in the freak accident and that the bombing mission was carried out successfully. The President did not care about the General, only about the fact that the Monk had been killed and his God destroyed, leaving him as a god of China and eventually a God of this world.

What the President did not consider was he was trying to take Satin's position as God/Ruler of the world, and that Satin would not surrender his position without a fight.

CHAPTER 38

While many considered Hong Kong to be a test of democracy, in reality, it was China who orchestrated the moves so it could judge the world's reaction to its takeover of Hong Kong. Many families, both who lived offshore and those who lived in China, had built up enormous wealth in Hong Kong over the years.

The Chinese Government did not know how other countries would react to China taking control of a democratic country and converting it back to communism. It did not want to be seen as the aggressor, even though it did not care what other countries really thought about Beijing. However, it did not want to be seen as dictatorial in its attitude and policies, causing other countries to reject China or refuse to do business with them. The one thing China wanted to avoid at all costs was sanctions being imposed on it and its wealthy families who owned property and businesses overseas and in China. Losing face was extremely important to the Chinese. Respect was what they sought and valued mostly.

To ensure that China was viewed as a reasonable minded country, it manipulated most of the movements and rallies for democracy and independence knowing that if these got out of hand, it would have no option but to move in and protect its citizens and businesses to ensure stability and peace within the country.

China recruited several citizens in Hong Kong that had been working in Hong Kong in finance and various strategic industries who had family back on the mainland in China. If those chosen co-operated, their families back home would not be harmed. However, if those chosen did not co-operate, their families would be imprisoned on cropped up charges. The State would confiscate all their assets and they would find themselves imprisoned, along with all of their family. If they co-operated, their families would not be touched and after they completed their assignment, they could either join their family in China or remain in Hong Kong.

All that they had to do was to go along with the demonstrations arranged by those who wanted democracy and freedom, and when the opportunity arose, ensure that confrontation and fighting took place with the authorities. The more aggressive the confrontation was, the better.

A simple task, as there would be a lot of hotheads willing to take up a fight against the police. It was starting one that was difficult as there were a lot of passive marchers who were prepared to come out and show their support for the cause and march in peace, but they were not prepared to start a fight or a skirmish. It would be up to those selected to throw the first punch and start the fight. After that, the authorities would move in and arrest all present. The bloodier the fight, the better, as it would show the size of the force needed to quell the uprising and to bring peace to the gathering.

As the demonstrations increased, more people came out in support and moved in solidarity with those demonstrating. Some held candles while other had placards calling for peace and democracy. Yet within the peaceful movement, there was a unit of those who were planted to disrupt the procession and cause anarchy. They removed barriers and accumulated Molotov cocktails to throw at police and army who would be sent in to regain peace and order.

The demonstrations build up to a crescendo and they brought in barriers to stop police moving in with water cannons to disburse the crowds. Police used rubber bullets to push the surging crowd back to no avail. They captured all this and the destruction and violence on television and screened the pictures worldwide to show that China had no alternative but to move in and regain law and order.

They sent the army in with orders to arrest anyone who did not behave or was intending to disrupt the demonstration. A curfew was established in Hong Kong and surrounding suburbs, and many were arrested and never to be heard of again. Many moved to other countries, taking up government schemes to allow citizens of Hong Kong to permanently relocate their families to those countries.

The army made sure that all those who objected to communism were dealt with, but they could film and show very little of this worldwide. China merely declared the world forced it to take control, which it did, to establish law and order.

This approach is the same now being used to control Taiwan. The only difference is China cannot send its militants to create a scene and move in to establish law and order. Taiwanese do not want Chinese involvement and declare themselves a democratic country. China will have to invade Taiwan if it wishes to annex the country and control it. The invasion will have to be in the form of an amphibious war for which the Taiwanese have prepared themselves for, over many years.

China knows that if it moved on Taiwan, it would incur world damnation and is prepared to take its time to ensure it is not left to fight the world and Taiwan. China looks as Russia invades Ukraine and the restrictions placed on that country for what they describe as an illegal invasion. The economy of Russia is put under extreme pressure and the country is isolated in its efforts to gain a military advantage. Europe and America join forces to support Ukraine and supply that country with advance weaponry to fight off the invaders. The war is a disaster from a humanitarian point of view, not that Russia cares about the lives of those innocent civilians nor their own men fighting a war that should have never started.

The United Nations calls for a ceasefire, which is ignored by Russia. Resolutions are voted upon in the United Nations. World condemnation is expressed but Russia still moves into Ukraine and bombards civilian areas on made up charges they are storing explosives. An excuse for killing innocent lives.

At home, Russia declares they have been invaded, and had no alternative but to defend themselves. For a while, the population believe their leaders but over time become suspicious over the lies being broadcasted on television.

The average Russian was being lied to daily as to why it invaded Ukraine. Most Russians knew they were being told lies, but did not care, as they held little regard or respect for the Ukrainians. They believed the Ukrainians were getting what they deserved and had little regard for them. Many innocent lives were being lost for no reason other than the President of the USSR wanting to take a window of opportunity to regain territory, which was lost some centuries ago.

The average Russian did not care about Ukrainian lives. It was the land that they were after. The raw materials that laid beneath the earth. It also gave them a buffer should anyone from Europe intend to invade Russia.

The Russians still had the historic concept that an invasion would most likely be by land, whereas this would not be the case. Invasions these days are more likely to be by the internet, missiles or by air. Drone warfare is most likely.

Very little was heard from the Russian people as to their opposition to the war or the number of civilian woman and children killed in the fighting. They wouldn't care, however, should the invasion backfire, they would come out to protest about the treatment inflicted on them and their country.

CHAPTER 39

While Russia invades Ukraine and the world inflicts economic sanctions as a reprisal, China gains more land and some small businesses in the Solomon Islands and negotiates a treaty with the island's prime minister to allow it to establish a naval base there where warships and other vessels can offload their cargo of military ammunitions and equipment.

The Prime Minister of the Solomon Islands continually shows his dislike for Australia and takes every opportunity to move closer to Beijing. The Australian's are criticised at every opportunity and Beijing praised for the smallest things.

The Solomon's overturned their support for an independent Taiwan, which they held for many years and declares in its opinion, Taiwan to be a State of China and agrees China should move on and take control of that country.

The Prime Minister of Solomon Islands supported China and made it clear he viewed America, England, and Australia to be more interested in their own plans than those to benefit the South Pacific.

Australia invests heavily in the development of Solomon Island by providing aid and peace-keeping forces to quell unrest and ensure the militant don't have their way.

China declares it sees its involvement in protecting its citizens and assets acquired on the island and continually invests heavily in the development of Honiara as a tourist destination. This was a ploy to allow it to drench the harbour on the pretext of bringing in heavy tourist cruisers to wharf there.

China did not state the truth, that it was drenching to allow its war ships to berth there, and not really caring about cruise ships.

The Prime Minister of the island allows China to take control of ensuring peace on the island and ask Australia to cease its involvement as the two countries have different views on law and order.

China shows its approach to demonstrations, as was the case in Hong Kong, which is to eliminate the force causing the disturbance. China establishes a group of militants to disturb the peace to ensure the police and army are called in to quell any uprising. Once this gets out of hand, the military is called in and from then on take control of the demonstrations and the Government.

The army crushes the opposing forces. However, in this case it can't send the people to imprisonment as it does in its own country as the Solomons operate under Rule of Law, so the Courts decide as to the punishment and not the ruling political party or the military.

The Chinese establish a military base near Honiara and have a naval presence permanently established on the island. They housed military personnel in separate quarters on the island and were very prominent in the streets of Honiara and the villages nearby.

Over time, China takes control of the country, as the island population has sold out their rights and now has nowhere to go. They fear that what is happening to Ukraine will happen to them. The only difference is that they cannot call upon America, Australia and Britain for help, as they have told them to leave and allow China to take control, which they regret.

If the Australian's were left to secure the island, this would not have happened as Australia was only there to keep the piece whereas China's plan from the start was to establish a military base there and take control of the island and its people.

The population could try to move to other islands being under the protection of Australia. However, there is no doubt that China has plans to use the Solomon Islands as a base to control what happens in the Pacific.

No other country will object or criticise China for fear that they would be dealt with harshly by the communist, so they say nothing, and hope Beijing will leave them alone.

As time goes on, the population becomes more and more wary of the Chinese and object to them buying up land and businesses. The riots become more intense as the population see that their freedom is restricted, and their island is no longer under their control. China has more say in running their country than they do. China invests heavily into the re-election of the Prime Minister and ensures that any opposition to his re-election is dealt with by force. There is continual and growing concern to rumours that the Prime Minister has been given substantial amounts of money by China for his continual support of them.

The opposing political party is against the Chinese and voice their objection to China taking control of the Solomon Islands. They campaign on the basis that all the land acquitted by China should revert to the State and China should hand over control of the island to the local police force and army.

Three days from the election, the opposition leader is found shot, but the election is allowed to proceed on the pretext that the population is electing a party and not an individual. Whoever wins can re-elect a new leader after the elections are over and run a by-election for the seat.

The current Prime Minister is re-elected and the population riot upon hearing this. The Chinese call out their military, who quells the riot and declares martial law with a six o'clock curfew.

All protesters are arrested but are freed by the courts as the Rule of Law still applies on the island.

China declares it has invaded the Solomons and therefore its laws apply throughout the land and not the Rule of Law. The Chinese government dictates to the judiciary what penalty is to apply and those who protest find themselves in jail or sent off to China to work in the mines. Never to return to their homeland.

The average islander protested too late at their government's sale of their lands and refused to see what the Chinese were doing to their country. They were happy to collect the money and snub those who were trying to help them and to see what would happen if they continued down the path of alienating themselves to a foreign power that did not have their best interest at heart and was intending to gain world dominance.

No one would now risk a war on behalf of the Solomon Islands and its population would serve their masters, the Chinese. The Prime Minister, who supported China and sold out to them, was found in his office with a bullet hole in his head. Many consider this should have happened a year or two earlier.

CHAPTER 40

America sees China taking over more of the islands in the Pacific and needs to make a stand as the world is moving closer to World War 3.

Congress meets and over several months debates its position in the conflicting world.

America declares it will abide by the NATO transatlantic alliance with Europe. However, declares a change in policy regards the Pacific. It declares it will not abide by any treaties made to assist any country other than the islands belonging to the United States. Therefore, it will protect the islands controlled by America such as Guam, Rota and American Samoa, but will not protect Australia, New Zealand, or Taiwan from invasion by the Chinese. It declares they have taken this decision with a realistic view of the capabilities of America and should these countries require American protection, they would have to become states of the United States.

None of the counties agreed to give up their sovereignty and were left to defend for themselves against China.

America declares that should China attack Taiwan or Australia, it would impose substantial restrictions on them, which would be far more severe than was placed on Russia. Unfortunately, the world looked at the restrictions placed on Russia and could not stop laughing as they were doing nothing in punishing Russia, who avoided these and still use its resources to fund the Ukrainian war. No doubt China could operate despite the restrictions and would still exert its substantial influence

China realised that if the restrictions were imposed, its economy would suffer and could cause the country's economy to collapse. A military win under these circumstances would achieve nothing, only a reduction in the population and an increase in the number who died in a theatre of war.

A meeting was called for by the National People's Congress to decide as to what China should do.

Most of the delegates became supporters of peace and could see that a war would achieve nothing other than the destruction of their economy and the killing of their youth. Most appealed for the vote to be against war. They knew to stand up against the Prime Minister's was a death threat and could cause them and their families to be killed. Nevertheless, more and more delegates stood up to support peace.

The Prime Minister seeing he would be outvoted and had little support from the delegates, decided to go to war before the vote was taken. He ordered the invasion of Taiwan to unify it with mainland China.

Taiwan, now not protected by America, and with a smaller army than that existed in China, would fall easily.

China sent a massive force from its mainland comprising fifty thousand men, two aircraft carriers, twenty destroyers, and two hundred plans with bombs and rockets.

The Taiwan military fired rockets at the incoming forces to eliminate the mass and could repel the first wave of bombers, but China knew where the rocket launchers were located and destroyed these quickly with rockets launched from mainland China and from fighter plans launched from carriers.

The Chinese military moved quickly to secure the airfields and stopped the Taiwanese from scrambling its air fighters. It also moved to control the ports and its destroyers blocked the shipping lanes, preventing any vessel from moving in or out of the ports. Taiwan was surrounded and could not launch fighters or allow any of its naval vessels to leave port. It was under a blockade.

Heavy carriers brought in tanks and a variety of vehicles with high calibre guns capable of destroying blockades and killing ground forces resisting the invading forces.

The Chinese used large transport planes to bring in troops, who moved quickly secured the infrastructure in the country, stopping communication and broadcast of news and updates on the war.

The Chinese killed many in invading Taiwan. They did not intend to take prisoners. The population was of no concern to them, as they expected a need for re-education to align with Chinese laws and customs. They marched those men who surrendered to a paddock and shot them at close range. China did not care about humanitarian objections as it knew no one would oppose its forces now that they have taken control of both Hong Kong and Taiwan.

Within two days, China secured the country and declared Taiwan to be under China's control. Taiwan's democracy was replaced by communism and the Rule of Law was given away to dictatorship.

They shut the television stations down and the only reception the population could receive was from China's mainland, which were lies and untruths as what had occurred.

Many Taiwanese families mourned the death of their loved ones and mourned the death of the sons and daughters who took up arms against the invaders however many were killed for no reason other than they resisted the military in their atrocious acts of raping woman and girls, destroying homes, structures and monuments the Taiwanese established in honour of their brave men and woman.

CHAPTER 41

It is Sunday and John Bishop moves into the pulpit and stares at the congregation.

John said, 'There is little doubt that war clouds are hovering over us, and the world has become a more dangerous place, with Russia and China planning to dominate the world.'

'Many have approached me, believing we will have to fight for our freedom and democratic rights, but are worried about what the bible says about killing. They have heard the words "Thou shall not kill" and wonder what they should do as they have been conscripted into the defence force and will be expected to kill the enemy.'

'To explain the current view of the church and society; I will first have to give you a broad view of how I see this very complex matter, which each of us will have to decide this point, if war breaks out or we are invaded.'

'Most people are unaware that as best as can be ascertained, approximately a little over four hundred thousand soldiers died in World War 11 and over half a million soldiers became behavioural health casualties. In fact, the number of combat stress casualties in World War 1, World War 11 and the Korea War was greater than the number of those who died in actual combat.'

'We cannot ignore that wars take their toll on more than just the physical bodies of those that serve. The truth is, returning from combat is more complicated than what those in power want us to believe. After living in warlike conditions, it is difficult to just flip a switch and return instantly to your old life. As the veterans of Iran and Afghanistan can vouch for.'

'The January 2005 edition of the Army Times noted that the first signs of Post Traumatic Stress Disorder (PTSD) may not appear until some four months after the soldier returns home.'

'What the soldier sees in war can rock one's theological concept of God and the way he works in the world. What many have witnessed makes no sense to them and therefore, God gets blamed for allowing such terrible things to happen. In times like these, people forget we are free willed and may adopt or reject good and evil and the by-product of evil is suffering. God didn't start the war. Men did this and men must end the war by earthly means and not through godly means.'

One question that has been asked regularly, 'Was Jesus strictly a pacifist who prohibited violence absolutely.' Some passages in the Bible seem clearly to imply this is the case, but other state the opposite.

'I will consider the Bible Position first.'

'In Matthew chapter 5, Jesus says, 'You have heard it being said, an eye for an eye and a tooth for a tooth. But I say to you, do not resist an evildoer. If anyone strikes you on the right cheek, turn and offer him the other one.'

'You have heard, you should love your neighbour and hate your enemy. But I say to you, love your enemies and pray for those who persecute you. These sayings seem to imply a strict rule of nonviolence and have inspired Christian pacifists for nearly two millennia. The passages rule out as illicit, all use of violence and injury against others and the participation in wars.'

'Yet Jesus spoke with Roman soldiers but never recommended that they abandon their profession to serve God.'

'Yet just because he was never reported to have criticised soldiers doesn't mean he supported their vacation.'

'The gospel further portrays Jesus as using force to eject merchants from the Temple in Jerusalem. It seems explicit that he permitted his disciples to carry swords and, by implication, to use them in self-defence. The book of Revelation depicts the returning Christ as a mighty worrier "Just in War" and wielding a sharp sword to smite the nations. The four Gospels agree that when Jesus was arrested by the Jewish Guards, one disciple drew a sword and cut off the ear of the high priest's servant. Jesus says, "Stop. He who lives by the sword shall die by the sword." In other words, if you don't want to be killed yourself, don't use lethal weapons. That is Jesus' position, but when we look at the Old Testament, we see God had angels kill forty thousand men in one night. God also become angry at those that he brought out of Egypt who worshipped idols and in front of Moses caused those who did not believe in him to perish. God also commanded Joshua to go into Canaan with an army of men to destroy the Canaanites. So, killing was not an isolated incidence in the Bible.'

'How did the early christian communities answer whether force could be morally justified?'

'Many of them seem to have affirmed a dual ethic, one for Christians and another for the State.'

'The disciple Paul wrote in Romans 12, 'Do not repay anyone's veil for evil. Beloved, never avenge yourself, but leave room for the wrath of God. Do not repay evil for evil.'

'Over a century after Paul, Tertullian wrote that when Jesus rebuked the disciples who defended him at his arrest, he disarmed every soldier. He also explained to Roman rulers that Christians believe it's better for them to be killed than to kill and that they may never retaliate if injured by others, and he stipulated that when soldiers converted to Christianity, they must leave the military. Origen also claimed that Jesus prohibited homicide, so Christians may never kill for any reason.'

'But all three early Christians thought God allowed the State to use lethal force for certain purposes. Paul wrote in Romans 13: 'Let every person be subject to the governing authorities; for there is no authority except from God, and those authorities that exist have been instituted by God. Therefore, whoever resists authority resists what God has appointed, and those who resist will incur judgement.'

'Cadoux concluded many other Christians shared the view and no Christian should simply assume that Jesus clearly approved of the use of violence, even in defence of the innocent. Killing enemies to protect one's family, community or nation might in fact be morally justified, but doing so may well contradict the ethic of Jesus.'

'However, a significant shift in Christian thinking about war occurred in the fourth and fifth centuries after Emperor Constantine used the Roman State to support the church.'

'According to an influential bishop named Eusebius, absolute nonviolence was from then on to apply solely to clergy, monks and nuns; lay Christians could now be obligated to defend the empire with force.'

'Ambrose, another important bishop of that era, thought that Christians love entailed a duty to use force to defend innocent third parties. He even claimed, 'He who does not keep harm off a friend, if he can, is as much at fault as he who causes it.'

'Christians in Augustine's view are not only permitted using force in defence of the community, but they're also obligated to obey such orders from higher authorities. However, Ambrose and Augustine also believed that there should be moral limits on Christian uses of violence. Even where Augustine considered war to be the lesser of evils, he regarded all killing as ultimately tragic, always requiring the Christian inflictor to have deeply regretted his actions.'

'During the medieval period, killing in war was considered a very serious sin, even if the bishop deemed it to be just. The person would have to do penance for the killing, often by fasting and praying for a year or more.'

'Aquinas added another important ethical consideration in stipulating that Christians may only use the minimal force needed to save lives from unjust attack. But the medieval period also witnessed the emergence of total war in the name of Christianity. First, there was the total glorification of the Christian knight and recognition of military courage and honour. But these restraints eroded in the medieval period.'

'In the ninth century, the Vatican declared that death in battle could be spiritually beneficial for Christian, in that their sins could be erased if they died in defence of the church, and they would be guaranteed entry into heaven.'

'In the year 1095, in response to a request from the Byzantine Emperor while fighting the Muslim enemies, Pope Urban 11 launched the First Crusade, urging knights to rescue the Holy Land from its infidel occupiers. From this point of time, killing Muslims became a way for Christians to get remission of their sins. Moral rules governing the conduct of war were abandoned. Captured Muslim soldiers and defenceless civilians were slaughtered following the capture of Jerusalem in the year 1099. Even Jews in Germany were massacred by the crusaders on the way to Palestine.'

'Tragically, a religion that began with the teaching of Jesus developed in its first millennium, where Christians waged indiscriminate war against their enemies.'

'It seems that the modern prohibition of killing stems from interpreting Jesus' saying in Matthew 26 that "All who take the sword will perish by the sword." Yet this has been interpreted in different ways: Tertullian in "On the Crown" interprets it as forbidding any use of force by Christians. Ambrose in Duties of the Clergy limits its prohibitive scope to killing in self-defence. Strange, as Peter was defending Jesus and not himself when he drew his sord to defend Jesus. Augustine, in Against Faustus, notes Jesus did not specifically authorise Peter to use the sword. Aquinas claimed Peter represented bishops and priests and Jesus was only forbidding Christian clergy from bearing arms. Yet the Russian Orthodox council of bishops concluded from Jesus's statement to mean "there is justification in the idea of just wars".'

'The thinking today revolves around who are you killing and under who's authority.'

'The "Who" refers to, are you going to kill another soldier who will kill you if you do not pull the trigger first? The reality is that the other soldier can drop his weapon and run, which means he should not be killed. He has the choice, as do you? If you kill him in line with your duty, then this is a sin but if you did it with remorse with no other alternative, then it is considered you are following orders and therefore the sin will not be held against you, but it will go to the cross.'

'If the soldier dropped his weapon and you could see he was unarmed, then you are killing an unarmed person if you press the trigger and cannot, under these circumstances, consider you were following orders. In plain language, you are a murderer and no better than Cain when he killed Abel.'

'If the person turned and ran from you and you internationally shot him in the back to kill him, thinking this will mean one less of the enemy, then again you are killing when it was unnecessary and not in self-defence, and the sin will be yours and for you to bear.'

'The matter of under whose authority are you acting upon is very important in this consideration and in wars. This question brings both religion and the State together. The religion aspect is that God gives the State authority and therefore he allows the action. The State comes in as the person takes up a position of authority within the State. It is the State that gives you the order theoretically with God's consent and blessing. The line of authority is from God to the State to the person in authority.'

'If they conscripted you, then some higher authority has ordered you into service and has trained you to kill. If this authority orders you into action, then you must obey the order and any killing or sin will be placed on the person who gave the order. Authority is an appointment from God and therefore, as long as you are following strict orders given to you, then the sin is not yours, but moves up the ladder of command and rests with the ultimate person who gave the order.'

'Modern thinking about killing at war rests on the question "Whose orders are you carrying out," and have you been acting totally within the scope of those orders? If you have, then the sin is accorded to the person ordering you into action and not yours. The sin moves up the line of command to the person who has the authority to give the order. Your responsibility is to follow the orders and not disobey them or become a conscientious objector.'

'God appoints all in authority. Therefore, you must not question their right to decide, but to follow orders and carry out what they have ordered you to do. The sin will lie with that person and not you, because God appointed that person and gave him the authority to command. Your job is to obey the orders without questioning, and therefore they bear the sin if they do not act in good faith and command you to do something unnecessary or to kill innocent souls.

'While your soul hurts from what you have done, and it was against your better judgement, you had no alternative but to follow those orders. You should then seek repentance from God.'

'You must act totally within the orders given to you and do not kill unnecessarily or wilfully and ask God for His help and support while in action.'

'To ease the mental traumatic experience that inflicts men and women, when they come from action, they must seek help from Jesus. Those who are not Christians will find this period a very lonely and hard road to walk on.'

'Many try to overcome their guilt by turning to drugs or alcohol, but they only find temporary relief and the problem is not addressed or goes away. Overtime their marriages break up as the wife and kids are subjected to violence and the household budget relies totally on the pension. It is only through Christ that you will find your answer and relief.'

Let us pray......

CHAPTER 42

America did not send troops to prevent the invasion of Taiwan. Instead, Congress and the Senate held meetings to vote on sanction to be imposed on China. These were debated in both houses and agreed to unanimously.

The sanctions were imposed on China, which included the cessation of countries selling goods to China or purchasing from China. All assets held in Europe, Australia, New Zealand, Canada, Scandinavian Countries and America were to be confiscated by the relevant country and became the property of that country. No banking was to be done with China and they were prevented from using the international banking system to transact currency exchanges.

China quickly found itself isolated and for a short period it supported itself, as they have a large population. However, they still needed to trade with the world, otherwise they would not develop and grow.

In the past, the Chinese could develop new products from innovations developed in the West. They did not have or recognised patents and therefore stole the technology invented in the western countries. Now it could not do this as it was not privileged to new products and was no longer manufacturing for the West and the developed countries. The local population, while large, could not absorb the loss of trade from the world, and China found its economy shrinking and would pick up pace as time went on.

The National People's Congress blamed the President for the situation as the Congress voted not to invade Taiwan, but he did it irrespective of their decision and now the country was paying for his poor decision.

Congress, after much debate, stood the President down and appoint a committee of three to run the country. The current president was not to have input in the day-to-day decisions.

The Committee met and over several weeks came up with a plan that it believed would resolve the current situation.

China would declare that they would withdraw all troops from Taiwan and would allow it to revert to a democracy. However, any newborn child would be taught as children on mainland Chinese are. This way the current occupants will still be allowed their freedom, and the newborn would be taught as the rest of Chine. Over a long period, the country would revert to the Chinese culture and adopt the law existing on the mainland. The rule of law will still apply to those who are currently in Taiwan. Newborn would be subject to the laws existing in China.

The President agreed to the demands of the Committee and was reinstated in his position to serve out his term.

The world, while not liking the situation, debated the decision made by the National People's Congress in the United Nations Assembly. Many countries like Australia and America preferred not to accept the decision of the Committee and protested over the reappointment of the existing president. However, the world needed China as China needed to trade with the world and finally the almighty dollar became the driving force that persuaded the Western Countries to accept the proposal.

While it did not achieve total independence of Taiwan, it allowed the current generation to live out their lives free with democratic rights while acknowledging China's right to regain and maintain sovereignty over its territory.

It was agreed that the current system of Rule of Law would last a maximum of one hundred years and that newborn would be subject to Chinese Laws.

Communist court would be established in Taiwan after fifteen years to allow those born as at the date of proclamation to be judged under Chinese Laws and schools were built to cater for the education of the newborn in line with mainland China's teachings.

Peace once again reverted to the country and over time, sanctions were lifted to enable the country to recommence trading with the world.

China still held onto its islands in the Pacific and Solomon Island was still governed by China, who hoped to adopt the same system as introduced into Taiwan, as most of the country was owned by the Chinese. The population could follow their democratic rights, but the newborn would be subject to the Chinese law and teachings did allowed for transferring culture.

Australian maintained its policy to secure a relationship with the islanders and paid substantial amounts to prevent the islanders transferring their allegiance to China.

Australia should have adopted a firm negotiating position, but instead maintained a position of trying to appease the Islanders no matter what problems they created. Australia should have held its ground and advised the islanders to either go with China and take the consequences or stay with Australia and maintain their independence.

The Chinese were visionary in their plan in that they handed over a lot more money to the island's administrators than Australia could do to secure its position. Once Australia was asked to leave and China took control, then it could recoup its investments and take total control of the islands and their people.

The administrators who sold their people out for sizeable sums of money tried to move to Australia, New Zealand, America, Europe, or Canada but were told, in no circumstances would they be welcomed in those countries.

Maney ended up in Africa where they were stripped of their wealth by the State with very little left to ensure a luxurious life, as they had planned.

CHAPTER 43

Australia was next in the firing line, with China declaring its citizens living in Australia were being badly treated and the assets China held in Australia were being put at risk.

The Chinese had secured several islands in the Pacific and had built airstrips on these and deepened the ports to ensure they could bring in supply ships, destroyers, and carriers.

Like Taiwan, Australia could not adequately defend itself from China's invasion. It had no missile defence system to intercept missiles being launched from warships in the Pacific and from the islands China had gained close to Australia.

China also had an agreement with Samoa and some of the larger islands in the Pacific, which enabled them to use their ports for military purposes and they could launch their invading forces from there. Samoa also enabled China to use its base to store supplies of ammunition, rockets, and supplies such as fuel and food.

The Samoans thought they were in control and could dictate to the Chinese what could or could not be done. The Chinese agreed to all the terms the Samoans wanted and paid a premium price for the facilities they secured.

The Chinese were leading the Samoans up the garden path, allowing them to think they were in control and shrewd negotiators. However, the Chinese knew that once they began their invasion of

Australia, Samoa would also fall to the Chinese and become a state of China.

China made sure that Samoa was under its control before commencing its invasion of Australia. All airstrips were secured by Chinese troops, who also controlled all transmission stations, power plants, radio and television stations. The islanders who resisted were shot, leaving many morning families wondering what their politicians had done in selling out to the Chinese. Samoa acted as if it was a mature country able to negotiate with the Chinese at their level, but it refused to accept advice from Australia, America and France that they were being conned by the Chinese, who would not uphold their side of any agreement.

Samoa, because of the action of its politicians, had let itself come under the control of the Chinese, who made it clear that the country would now become a province of China.

Australia had a large Chinese population who had kept advising China of the military buildup that was occurring and sending back to China pictures of ports and facilities that were being used for military purposes. In short, they acted as spies for the Chinese Government. Now they had the upper hand and were supporting China in its invasion of Australia.

Workers at the Chinese dairy farms and cotton farms also advise China of what was happening in Australia and relayed news broadcasts back to China.

Australia could not defend itself against the military power of China and fell to the invading forces after three days of heavy fighting. The unthinkable became a reality in China dominating the Pacific. Countries like Indonesia and Malaya becoming neutral and agreed to support China.

China took control of Australia's airports and military bases and ports. It already had control of Darwin's port when it purchased the right on a ninety-nine-year lease.

The major cities in Australia were overrun by Chines troops and many citizens were shot where they stood for no reason other than they were being invaded and to send a message back to those who opposed the invasion that they were confronting a well-disciplined, well-trained army capable of inflicting a lot of pain on those who resisted them. China was taking over and would not tolerate any opposition or disrespect.

The Chinese brought in tanks and other military equipment to kill off any resistance quickly and secured the cities and major towns quickly.

China did not care about the population of Australia. It invaded Australia is it wanted the Taiwanese microchip facilities, Australia's raw materials and the space facilities established by the Americans in Australia. It did not want the population. It had enough people back in China and did not require more.

Australians were treated as second-class citizens in their own country. The Chinese considered themselves far superior to the Australians as their country prospered and they sold no portion of their land to foreigners, as Australia had done on the pretext of receiving investment.

Australia was forced to give up its democracy and adopt Communism. Those who protested found themselves in prison or shot dead, ending their resistance or any protest that was mounted.

The Greens and other protestors were shot as they marched in protest; their bodies were dumped in a mass grave in the Hunter region in a large excavation site owned by one of the mining companies.

The Chines established coal-fired plants to gain a base load of electricity to ensure viability of industry. Those who objected on the grounds of climate change were imprisoned for three months without electricity (except electricity generated by wind turbines, which gave at best, five minutes a day of electricity, and after that there was darkness).

Australians had no rights in their own country, leading to forces being formed for guerrilla warfare. These forces were not affective against the well equipped Chinese troops, who could order in rockets, drones, tanks and any other form of equipment to eliminate any resistance.

The aboriginal objection to the invasion was dealt with swiftly by shooting those who objected. Soon this movement ceased as most understood they would not find the Chines a soft target as were the Australians, and since there was no likelihood of treaties or compensation, they kept quiet, and never protested based on invasion etc,. as they had done for years previously.

Heavy casualties were incurred by the Australian forces in its efforts to resist Chinese aggression.

Many who were trained who had left the army as reserves, quickly moved to the bushlands and mountains area, away from the main areas of the invading forces, which in the main were in the cities and larger regional towns where the main industry was mining and the shipping ports on the coastal areas.

The forces could hit the enemy hard with guerrilla warfare tactics when they leased expected it. The Chinese shot many of the locals, as they refused to divulge the location of the of the resistance movement. Emphasis was on disrupting the Chinese supply chains, slowing their movement down and preventing them from advancing, but this was only causing a nuisance factor as China had many armed men on the ground and they were being supported by fighter planes and helicopters.

China's friend, chairperson of Fortescue Metals Ltd was appointed Administrator of Australia by the Chinese National People's Committee and the former prime minster of Australia a socialist and a friend of China, his deputy.

The war lasted four years, and many lost loved ones and all that they possessed in the fighting.

Those who had previously supported the Chinese were treated harshly as the Chinese looked at them with contempt and could not trust them. They turned their backs on a Democratic system and thought they would get special privileges from the Chinese. They found out firsthand what the Chinese were like when it came to matters of human rights.

CHAPTER 44

J apan, who was a historic enemy of the Chinese, was next in line. They had built up a powerful fleet of naval vessels and war planes and could defend themselves against the Chinese. With America's support, they could prevent their country from being invaded and inflicted a lot of damage on the Chinese cities through a prolonged campaign of bombings crippling the Chinese manufacturing centres.

America also became more aggressive against the Chinese, weakening their capabilities through missiles and bombing strikes. The Chinese suffered heavy losses in the destruction of naval warships and submarines through bombing attaches by both the Japanese and American bombing attaches.

The Chinese relied on rocket attaches on Japan, which were not affective as Japan had the American ground to air missile system which intercepted and destroyed most of the Chinese missiles.

In Europe, they had their hands full in fighting against Russia and North Korea, who underestimated the power of the European countries and the sophistication of their weaponry, plus the manpower in a combined front. Because of this, America could devote more resources to fighting the Chinese in the Pacific, leaving the European countries to handle Russia's and Korea's attacks.

Throughout the Chinese' attack the Japanese knew of the hatred the Chinese had for them, which stemmed back even prior to the second world war. The relationship between the countries was cordial but mostly each had frequently declared hostility towards the other.

CHAPTER 45

The UN National Assembly came to order and the Chairman readout the motion that was to be voted on. Those counties who wanted to speak took turns throughout the day to present their case and advised how they would vote. Many heated arguments were declared, with China's delegates objecting to the actuations expressed on the floor. They declared they always acted with concern of the individual and abided by the Human Rights Charter.

All who wanted to speak had their say. The Chairman moved the motion which criticised China, and each delegate was to vote on the motion.

After about half an hour, the Chair declared that all had voted and that the vote was seventy-five percent in favour of China.

The news broadcasters carried the story that China was found not to be in breach of its Human Rights obligation according to world opinion.

No mention was made of China's invasion of the Pacific Islands or Australia. No one wanted to experience the wrath of China and when the motion was raised about China's aggressive action in the Pacific, the Chairperson advise this was not on the agenda and therefore could not be raised or debated.

Everyone knew this was not the case and that the vote was paid for by China, and therefore looked towards the decision from the International Human Rights Commission.

The Chinese President gave instruction to his group of assassins that Sue and her team were not to make the presentation nor arrive in Netherlands.

Sue was sitting at her desk when she received an email from Jerry advising her of the UN resolution. Jerry also informed Sue that the Barrister employed to present the case to the Commission had been involved in a fatal car accident and therefore would not appear on their behalf. Another person would have to be sought that would take the matter on.

Sue knew that no one would take the matter on and that it would be left to her to present the case, as she and her team were the only one who knew the arguments and the evidence that was to be presented. Also, that there was little time left to brief anyone else. She emailed Jerry that she would take her team to Netherlands and present the case herself to the International Human Rights Commission. She did not wait for confirmation from Jerry but filed the Notice of Appearance with the Commission through the internet, advising them she would present the case.

The Commission supported her application and noted the danger involved. They sent a formal letter to the President advising him they would hold China and him personally responsible should anything happen to Sue and her team as they viewed the demise of witnesses and presenters more than suspicious and urging on criminality.

Sue was in her room, going over her notes, making sure nothing would be missed. The procedure she had to follow was first she had to make an opening statement, setting out her argument against the Chinese. Second, she had to present the evidence and witnesses and examine them under oath before the court. Finally, she had to sum up her argument and thirdly declare what she is seeking from the court in the way of punishment.

She put her notes down for a minute and riminess' the conversation she just had with her sister Irene, who was in a safe house with the children back in the States. She was thankful they were not with her as she could not concentrate on her presentation while worrying whether someone was going to shoot them or one of the kids as they threatened they would. As she was deep in thought, a knock at the door brought her back to reality. The person on the other side yelled out, Jerry, we are ready to go off to the court. Sue grabbed her notes and bag and opened the door. Jerry said, 'Well are you ready?' Sue replied, 'Ready as I will ever be.'

The police were downstairs waiting for everyone to assemble so they could escort them to the Court. Once everyone was there, they radioed the police outside that they were coming out and moved one by one initially, then by twos. Each person was told which vehicle they were to go to, and each moved in an orderly manner.

Next was Jerry's and Sue's turn. They moved out of the building and momentarily stopped to see which vehicle they were to go to when a shot rang out and Jerry slumped to the ground bleed from a hole just below his heart. The police returned fire, but the shooter opened fire again, hitting two policemen in the chest. Sue ran to the car and crouched down so the shooter could not see her. She could see Jerry on the ground from the opened door and he looked as if he was dead. He was not moving at all. The police ran to the building from where the shoots had been fired the shot, but the shooter had escaped. The ambulance was called, and they arrived within minutes, putting Jerry onto a stretcher, and giving him oxygen and collecting the other two shot policemen. It was only minutes to the hospital who were alerted as to what had happened and were ready to take the injured into surgery.

Sue was rushed off with an escort to the Court and was rushed into the basement care park to ensure the shooter didn't have a second go at killing her.

The Court was informed of the shooting of Jerry. Chief Justice said, 'We understand that the case cannot be presented by Mr Wright Barrister KC. The second presenter has been shot and currently is undergoing surgery in hospital. Are you able to present your case or do you wish for us to stand it down to enable you to brief an appropriate person to present it?'

Sue rose to her feet and moved to the bar table. She said, 'While there has been an attempt to silence us, those ordering the killings will not stop us proceeding with our case. I will handle the case myself and am prepared to begin on your instruction.'

The Chief Justice looked at the panel of judges present and then said, 'We will allow you to make the presentation, so please biggin.'

Sue took out her notes and adjusted the microphone to her height and said, 'Your Honour, our case is against the Government of China and in particular, the National People's Committee in that country. They have ordered the abuses and denied Human Rights to several countries and their people. While we cannot present a case for all those affected or illegally imprisoned, we argue that the Uyghurs Muslims living in Xinjiang in northern China and the citizens of Hong Kong have been denied human rights. We also state the invasion of the Pacific Islands and Australia has also shown China's lack of concern for human rights in those who have protested have been shot without trial or appearance in a court. Many have been imprisoned on charges that are politically driven rather than based on evidence and they have been denied their freedom or day in court.'

'There are approximately twelve million Uyghurs Muslims living in Xinjiang which is officially known as the Xinjiang Uyghur Autonomous Region (XUAR). They speak their own language and ethnically are close to Central Asian nations. They make up approximately half of the population living in Xinjiang. Over the last three decades, there has been a migration of Han Chinese into Xinjiang to dilute the majority there.'

'China is accused of targeting Muslim religious figures and banning religious practices, as well as destroying mosques and tombs. It is feared that the culture is under threat of obliteration.'

'China has imprisoned at least 630 imams since 2014 in its crackdown in the region. Eighteen clerics had died in detention. The clerics are charged for preaching or officiating at prayer sessions, convene prayer groups or attending to duties expected of an imam such as officiating at marriage ceremonies. Recent three hundred and four clerics were judged by the courts. Sixty percent were sentenced to five years' imprisonment, twenty-six percent to twenty years or more of imprisonment, and fourteen received a life sentence.'

'It is clear China is attempting to break the religious tradition of the Uyghurs and assimilate them into Han Chinese Culture. China denies these allegations stating the re-education program is to stamp out extremism among the Uyghurs.'

'We accuse China of human rights abuses in the region, including slavery, sterilisation, and rape. Most Uyghurs are held in prison like camps, which are referred to as 're-education facilities' while others are given formal sentences.'

'In the main, the charges raised by China are based on a 'flimsy legal basis which do not qualify as offences. The real reason imams are targeted is because of their ability to bring people together in the community. The purpose is to restrict Uyghur culture and religion. Accused and sentenced Uyghurs are sentenced to lengthy sentences in prison without the right of appeal or to be formally advised in writing of the charge or sentence levied by the court. The court is only a mouthpiece for the State and does what is dictated to them.'

'The Chief Justice interrupted Sue and said, 'The matter of the Uyghurs has been brought before the Court by other groups and individuals. A decision is pending in those cases. We note that the People's Republic of China has not made a representation in this matter, nor have they lodged a written submission. Please go on to your next point.'

'Sue shuffled her papers and got to the next main point that being the Human Rights abuses in Hong Kong.'

Sue said, 'The transfer of the territory of Hong Kong occurred in 1997 when the United Kingdom's lease expired. China was adamant that it would not allow the lease to be extended, nor would it allow Hong Kong to gain independence. People organised protests about the Chinese occupation of the Territory, with about 100,000 people marching at one point. The Chinese authorities arranged for military personnel to join the march to specifically create havoc. This they did as a show of violence against the authorities contrary to the intentions of the organises. Those that ended up acting against the authorities were jailed, with some taken back to mainland China, never to be heard of again. Others received lengthy jail sentences for participating in the protest. They couldn't object and their family was sometimes punished because of their actions and were taken into custody.'

Sue continued with the outline of her case and on the second and third day, could have several witnesses appear in the witness box and give evidence as to what had happened to them and their family.

She continued on day four, presenting other evidence of human rights abuse by China and also present evidence from individuals and organisations to support her arguments of abuse.

On the fifth day, Sue summoned up her case and gave her final arguments to the Court. The Chief Justice said, 'We of the Bench, thank you for presenting this case to us for deliberation and judgement. We will defer our decision until all justices have considered the evidence.'

With that, all rose to their feet while the Justices left the Court. All personnel and reporters then made their way out of the courtroom. As Sue left the Court room, two TV stations interviewed her about the evidence presented.

CHAPTER 46

The Chinese President recalled it was Sue and her Human Rights Commission application and the Monk at the Eastern Province with his invisible God that gave him the most trouble. He had now become powerful and will get rid of Sue shortly and possibly the International Human Rights Commission.

He assumed the Monk had been destroyed years ago when he gave the order, and since then, things have been going right, so the Monk and is God have left him alone and he assumes was destroyed.

Sitting in his chair, he couldn't stop thinking about whether the Monk made it out alive from the bombing. He decided to go and see for himself and ordered a helicopter with support soldiers to accompany him the next morning. He cancelled his morning meetings and attended to some work and went to bed.

The next morning after breakfast, he was airborne to the Eastern Province. After flying for an hour, he arrived at the outskirts of the province and was surprised to see the church still standing. It had not been destroyed, as his generals had told him. He immediately ordered a drone attack on the church and would see for himself that his orders were carried out.

About fifteen minutes latter two drowns appeared over the horizon en route towards the church. They both slammed into the old building, demolishing it. The President was thrilled and ordered everyone back to base.

The Monk was in his church praying when he heard an enormous explosion some distance away and immediately got up to see what had happened. He could see smoke was billowing from the distance and decided to investigate. He took one truck that was parked in the village. Some villages got in, and he drove off towards the smoke on the horizon.

Ten minutes later, they stopped in front of their old church, which was in rubbles. This church was the first to be built by the villagers some fifty years ago was still standing but not secure. They could not understand why the building was bombed and stayed looking at the rubble for some time, not having any answers to their questions. They all left the building and went back to the village, deciding to leave the matter rather than inquire as to why the military bombed their building.

The president was very pleased, thinking he had got rid of the Monk and his God. Two weeks later, he entered the National People's Assembly and when the time came, stood up to declare that he had witnessed the destruction of the church some fortnight ago and could only assume the Monk and his God were both destroyed in the surprised bombing. Therefore, they did not have to worry about floods and pests being inflicted on them and could secure their position as the God of this earth.

One delegate stood up and said he had just come back from the Eastern Province yesterday after talking to the Monk and the church was still standing and the Monk very much alive. He went there to see if they could harvest more crops, as some provinces were still affected by the floods.

The President turned white and did not know what to say. He saw the church being bombed with his own eyes. He could only assume it was like the Monk being shot. The building must have miraculously reformed itself back into the shape it originally was before bombing, meaning it could never be destroyed.

The President thought about it; that meant the Monk, who could not also be killed, was still alive and he would now inflict more curses against them. He could not allow this to happen. The church must be destroyed to ensure no religions were practiced in China. The only worship allowed was the worship of the President.

The President decided he had to go back and finish the job. Everyone was looking at the President as he left the Assembly and many of the delegates commented on the fact that he was mumbling to himself and seemed to have lost co-ordination and realism.

The President called his generals in and advised he wanted the church destroyed that day in the Eastern Province. He did not care how it was done, but it needed to be done right away.

The Generals pointed out they would send in a demolition team in a few days to blow up the building. The President would not hear of the delay and wanted it done right away.

The generals pointed out that there was a cyclone in the China Sea which would make landfall within the next few days and the wind factor would prevent the building being bombed or drones being sent in. A rocket attack could go astray and kill innocent villagers. The President stood up and said, 'I don't care about the villagers. You can kill every one of them just bomb the church.'

The generals said they would attend to it immediately, knowing that it would be a few days before they could do the job. The President accepted their word and walked out of his office, leaving them there to discuss what and how they were going to accomplish the task.

The cyclone the Generals mentioned picked up speed and hit the Chinese Navil Base, smashing six ships, causing each to explode and sink to the bottom of the ocean. Cyclone made land and headed towards Beijing. Navel destroyers tied up at port were uplifted and taken in land just thrown around is if they were toys. In its path were airfields and other ports containing worships and submarines moored. The planes were ripped apart as if they were confetti and thrown around, destroying airfields, hangers and landing runways as planes burst into a ball of flames.

The cyclone ripped through villages and uprooted trees, buildings and any structure in its path. It reached Beijing and headed for the Assembly building, causing first the roof and then the walls to collapse on delegates who were sheltering there from the cyclone.

The President was at home, and his house was totally lifted from its foundations with all his family in it. They were never found presumably dumped into the sea some hundreds of miles from shore. The only thing found was the scarf the monk gave the President when he his pistol flew up in his hand when he tried to kill the monk.

As the cyclone passed the military bases, it smashed vessels into each other, causing explosions midships, as each was projected onto or against the adjourning vessel. Airplanes parked near the tarmac, where lifted and smashed into the tarmac and buildings nearby causing them to explode and as they progressively caught fire, they caused the buildings to catch fire and eventually burning them to the ground leaving a heap of twisted steel and concrete.

The mighty Chinese Navy was destroyed, as was their air force. It was as if a mighty hand had grabbed the planes and toss them around. The country could not now attack anyone as the only vessels they had were the ones tied up in port at the Solomon Island, which amounted to two frigates.

China was destroyed and could no longer force its will on other countries as it had previously done. The State would no longer be considered a god in the eyes of its people and the destruction showed what would happen should other nations again try to usurp authority from the legitimate God.

CHAPTER 47

S ue sat at her desk in her office noting the number of calls she was receiving from potential clients worldwide regards Human Rights abuses and her submissions to the International Human Rights Commission as she had done.

She noted that most were coming from African nations and countries that were under dictatorship or Communist countries. She took on the cases and over the years gained a reputation for defending freedom and human rights.

After five years, Sue was invited to become a judge of the International Human Rights Commission replacing a retiring member. Her expertise from Hong Kong demonstrations and need to flee to a new country and ensuing escape from the Chinese assassins coupled with her specialisation in the area gave her the training to sit on the bench of the International Human Rights Commission and eventually become Chief Judge of the Court.

One thing Sue learnt from her experience both in Hong Kong and on the bench was that democracy is something that has to be fought for, as there will always be someone trying to limit it or take it away from you. Even in countries that declare themselves to be democratic. Once that happens, it leads to human rights issues, and the injustices directed by a dictator who rules the courts and enslaves the people.

The other aspect that Sue noted was as a prerequisite to dictatorship, there occurred the elimination of religion as what China was doing with the Uyghurs Muslims. For if there is no greater power than the dictator, then you give the population no hope of overcoming the repression, as in China.

In these instances, the State takes the place of the church and religion; the Bible, being the word of God, is replaced by the dictators' decrees.

People in democratic countries may not realise that their government is implementing policies on sensitive topics such as abortion, euthanasia, and religion classes at schools being replaced with ethics classes. This is where it starts and before you know it, your democratic rights are restricted, which in reality affords no rights to the individual.

www.ingramcontent.com/pod-product-compliance
Lightning Source LLC
Chambersburg PA
CBHW021627120626
46545CB00002B/437